PLAYS BY RICHARD NELSON, EARLY PLAYS VOLUME TWO

BROADWAY PLAY PUBLISHING INC
56 E 81st St., NY NY 10028-0202
212 772-8334 fax: 212 772-8358
http://www.BroadwayPlayPubl.com

PLAYS BY RICHARD NELSON, EARLY PLAYS VOLUME TWO

First printing: December 1998
ISBN: 0-88145-151-7

Book design: Marie Donovan
Word processing: Microsoft Word for Windows
Typographic controls: Xerox Ventura Publisher 2.0 PE
Typeface: Palatino
Copy-editing: Liam Brosnahan
Printed on recycled acid-free paper and bound in the USA

CONTENTS

PLAYS BY RICHARD NELSON

ACCIDENTAL DEATH OF AN ANARCHIST, *adaptation of Dario Fo*
AN AMERICAN COMEDY*
BETWEEN EAST AND WEST*
CHESS, *libretto*
COLUMBUS AND THE DISCOVERY OF JAPAN
CONJURING AN EVENT*
DON JUAN, *adaptation of Molière**
THE FATHER, *adaptation of Strindberg**
IL CAMPIELO, *adaptation of Carlo Goldoni**
THE GENERAL FROM AMERICA
GOODNIGHT CHILDREN EVERYWHERE
JITTERBUGGING: SCENES OF SEX IN A NEW SOCIETY*
JUNGLE COUP*
THE KILLING OF YABLONSKI*
LIFE SENTENCES
THE MARRIAGE OF FIGARO, *adaptation of Beaumarchais**
MISHA'S PARTY, *written with Alexander Gelman*
NEW ENGLAND
PRINCIPIA SCRIPTORIAE
RIP VAN WINKLE, OR "THE WORKS"*
ROOTS IN WATER*
SCOOPING*
SENSIBILITY AND SENSE
SOME AMERICANS ABROAD
THREE SISTERS, *adaptation of Anton Chekhov**
TWO SHAKESPEARIAN ACTORS

**Published by Broadway Play Publishing Inc*

INTRODUCTION

Conversations with Richard Nelson lead inevitably to two topics: theater and politics. Nelson's anger and occasional pleasure in the political fortunes of his country are deeply felt. Discourse is essential to his insight, and the news of the day can obsess him. He is not without hope, but sees the gap between America's lofty goals and its day-to-day reality as an unacceptable burden of citizenship. America's successes are self-evident to him. Our national failures are what he chooses to confront through the shattered myths, ironic humor and violent imagery of his political plays. Believing that theater and civic argument are not mutually exclusive, he will sacrifice audience ease to confrontational issues: Nelson's political plays can be wilfully disturbing events on stage.

This volume contains three of Richard Nelson's earliest political dramas. Like the works in Volume One of this series, these plays chart the evolution of Nelson's prolific career as well as his evolution as a major American playwright. THE VIENNA NOTES was first produced Off-Broadway in 1979. Although well-received, it was the fourth Richard Nelson play to be staged in New York in a single year. Its production marked the end of Nelson's presence as a young writer in that city. His next phase of work took place in the inevitably nomadic world of American regional theater. BAL (following CONJURING AN EVENT) was first staged in Williamstown, Massachusetts in 1979, and in Chicago in 1980. THE RETURN OF PINOCCHIO had a 1982 workshop at San Francisco's Bay Area Playwrights Festival, and a full production at Seattle's Empty Space in 1983.

The decentralization of America's not-for-profit theater community beyond New York reached its most expansive period in these years. Nelson was soon a part of that movement and achieved prominence among playwrights in Washington, Chicago and on the West Coast. New artistic affiliations took root for Nelson, and he welcomed the opportunity to be a playwright-in-residence, influencing the work of theater companies that engaged him. In the course of the next decade, Nelson would become an Associate Director of the Goodman Theater in Chicago, and the literary manager of two important repertory companies: the BAM Theater Company in Brooklyn, and the Guthrie Theater in Minneapolis. From these experiences came his extended collaborations with stage directors Gregory Mosher, David Jones and Liviu Ciulei.

The political plays of those years mark Nelson's intense response to America's evolution from its left-leaning Post-Watergate era to the 1980 election of Ronald Reagan and the country's turn to the right. Outrage is the tone of voice that unifies much of his work from this period. Taken together, these three plays present a downward moral trajectory. THE VIENNA NOTES shows a politician who literally lives by acting, almost in opposition to reality. BAL (loosely based upon Brecht's first play) presents a defiantly evil character whose immoral rampage has political overtones. The sequence ends with THE RETURN OF PINOCCHIO, in which the familiar Italian folk tale becomes a dangerous Reaganite nightmare.

All three plays present victims without redemption—manipulative "players" who are blind to reality and mired in egotism. Nelson warns us about personal and political indulgence, and the threat of greed and selfishness when pitched as a defining social standard.

THE VIENNA NOTES continues the line of reporter plays presented in Volume One, but reverses the basic situation: instead of an egotistical scribe who confuses himself with his subject matter, the play's subject (a U S senator abroad) becomes the manipulative chronicler of his own life. Even in a murderous hostage crisis, Senator Stubbs lives only to exaggerate reality so that his self-serving memoir can become a best-seller. As in THE KILLING OF YABLONSKI, murder and terrorism are buried beneath the needs of selfish ego. Stubbs and those around him become out-of-control performers who replace their lives with acting games. But this time, going beyond the scope of YABLONSKI and JUNGLE COUP, Nelson raises the thematic stakes. His target becomes not just the excesses of American journalism, but the way immorality intersects with our politics and election process.

BAL represents a considerable break with Nelson's previous work. Assuming the title of Brecht's early play, this is the first Nelson drama to echo styles and even characters from both modern and classic theater. From this starting point will come many Nelson adaptations, including Brecht's JUNGLE OF THE CITIES. The emergence of BAL, with its contemporary American sensibility tempered by Brechtian irony, made Nelson an inspired choice for the literary manager jobs he would soon hold.

BAL begins very much in the mode of THE VIENNA NOTES and JUNGLE COUP: a reporter taking notes for a magazine profile is enchanted with the aggressively verbal man he's interviewing. But the play soon moves into a new style, one quite different from what Nelson employed up to this time. Some of the change is in his use of classic Brecht techniques, as when a character declares his greatest optimism at the moment he commits suicide. Building upon Nelson's established form, the anticipated manipulation among characters in BAL becomes far more extreme, explicit and violent.

BAL can be hard to take, and not just because of its gutter imagery. Its ruthless, confessional language is more naturalistic than anything Nelson wrote previously. Its ease makes it credible. For the first time, his verbal gift expands beyond its initial style, one best defined by the somersaulting imagery of CONJURING AN EVENT. In BAL, the playwright knows that he need not be an acrobat—the characters become more disturbing by restraining their verbal athletics. There is less humor, greater agony, and subtler references to the confused threats of political abuse.

With THE RETURN OF PINOCCHIO, Nelson's fury at Reaganism takes center stage. The puppet who became a real boy, one whose nose grew when he lied, is now a Hollywood star, thanks to Disney's cartoon film of the 1940s. Pinnochio returns to his Italian village after World War II, only to find poverty and corruption. His response is to become an "Ugly American"—one very much in line with the nationalistic jingoism of Reagan's America. As in BAL, Nelson doesn't hesitate to surround his play with violent images, but it's all to illuminate moral outrage at the contemporary events of the playwright's own time.

Robert Marx is Executive Director of the New York Public Library for the Performing Arts.

BAL

BAL is for Marty Kapell and Jennifer Tipton

BAL was first presented by The Williamstown Second Company in the summer of 1979, directed by Martin Kapell.

BAL was produced subsequently by The Goodman Theater (Gregory Mosher, Artistic Director) on 6 March 1980. The cast and creative contributors were:

BAL .... Jim Belushi
JOHNNY .... Cosmo White
SOPHIE .... Caitlin Clarke
JOHANNA .... Lora Staley
DUSZAK .... Del Close
EMILY DUSZAK/FEMALE SINGER .... Patricia Hodges
PLANTER/CRAP-PLAYER .... Michael Saad
ZEIGLER/PRIEST/CRONY .... John E. Mohrlein
YOUNG WOMAN .... Ellen Crawford
MAN/MAN WITH FISHING POLE .... Dennis Kennedy
YOUNG MAN .... Leland Crooke
MAN WHO ACTS LIKE BEAST/WAITER .... Daniel Cooney
MAN WHO ACTS LIKE BEAST/BOSS .... Ron Dean
GUEST .... Belinda Bremner

Director .... Gregory Mosher
Costumes .... Dunya Ramicova
Lights .... Jennifer Tipton

Scene One (a)

(A field. Night. BAL *(thirties) and* JOHNNY *(early twenties) lie on their backs looking at the stars. Johnny has a notepad. Music in the distance. Pause.)*

JOHNNY: I took your advice and talked to Johanna. *(No response)* My girl?

BAL: Oh. And...?

JOHNNY: And nothing. We talked. Or rather she did. She claims it has nothing to do with me, and if she were to go to bed with anyone, it would certainly be with me. But right now, she has a lot of things to figure out about herself. She says, she wants to know who she is before getting too involved in anything.... I don't know. I can wait, if that's what she wants; that is, if I have to. But, Jesus Christ, I don't know. What do you think, Bal? She's only sixteen.

BAL: What do I think?

*(*JOHNNY *nods.)*

BAL: I think many things, Johnny. One moment this. The next something else. Some of my thoughts are pretty stupid. Some are fantastic. Some have changed my life. Others have bored me to tears. I think a lot of things. Bal does. *(Short pause—looks back at the stars)* Is it wrong to want to feel?

JOHNNY: *(Opening up his notepad, set to write)* Go ahead, Bal, I'm listening.

BAL: *(Continuing his thought)* I mean, in a certain way, I wish we didn't know what we know, or maybe that what we knew we found out was wrong. How I would love to look up at the stars and the moon and say—"what fools we were to think that we were spinning; to think that we were on an earth which revolves." I would love to pity the poor scientists. I would love to once again believe that we were at the center of things, that all moved around us. Then I wouldn't feel like I was missing something. Then I wouldn't be bothered by not being able to feel us moving. If we are spinning, is it really wrong to want to feel it? And if I can't feel it, I'd rather not know we were moving at all.

JOHNNY: Beautiful, Bal.

BAL: *(Getting up)* That's enough of that for tonight.

JOHNNY: I can hardly wait to finish this profile. The notes I've already submitted, you can't imagine what a stir they've created. My editor's even talking about a cover, Bal.

BAL: Listen. *(We hear the music in the distance.)* That party won't last forever. Come on, I need a drink. *(He starts to go.)* I want to feel myself spinning.

Scene One (b)

*(*DUSZAK*'s dining room. Music. Food. Drink.* DUSZAK, *a wealthy businessman;* EMILY DUSZAK, *his attractive wife;* ZIEGLER, *an employee;* PLANTER, *a servant;* YOUNG MAN; YOUNG WOMAN; *and* MAN *(guests). Also* JOHNNY *and* BAL, *who sits at a table and eats.)*

DUSZAK: Planter, another bottle of Bordeaux!

PLANTER: Yes, Mr Duszak. *(Hurries out)*

DUSZAK: I can tell, Ziegler, that you think Old Duszak's being a bit extravagant.

ZIEGLER: I wasn't thinking anything of the kind, sir. Though there are but four or five bottles of Bordeaux left in the cellar.

DUSZAK: I know perfectly well what is and what is not in my own cellar, Ziegler. So there are only four or five bottles of Bordeaux left. The question is, Ziegler, *why* are they left?

ZIEGLER: Why, sir?

DUSZAK: Because I have been hoarding them. And why have I been hoarding them, Ziegler?

ZIEGLER: Why, sir?

DUSZAK: For a reason, that's why. And what sort of reason am I suggesting, Ziegler?

ZIEGLER: What, sir?

DUSZAK: For a *very good* reason, that's what. Ziegler, man has reasons for what he does. He has a mind. He thinks. He reasons. I am a man. I have a mind, I think. So I have my reasons!

ZIEGLER: I'm sure you must, sir.

DUSZAK: *And* if I have my reasons for hoarding my Bordeaux, then it is fair to assume that I have my reasons for uncorking it as well. Ziegler, man thinks. Man has new thoughts. Man changes his mind. And man finds new reasons! And what sort of reasons must a man find to change his mind?

ZIEGLER: I give up, sir.

DUSZAK: Very good reasons, that's what!!

ZIEGLER: Makes sense, sir.

DUSZAK: And what could be a better reason than... *(Waves his arms, pointing out the room)*

ZIEGLER: Than what, Sir?

DUSZAK: *(Yelling)* Mr Bal!!!

EVERYONE: *(Stopping their chitchat and toasts)* To Mr Bal!!!

BAL: Pass the sausage plate, please. *(He eats.)*

YOUNG WOMAN: *(Slightly drunk)* Mr Duszak, would you tell us again how you found our guest of honor?

MAN: *(To* YOUNG MAN*)* I love this story, don't you?

*(*YOUNG MAN *and* MAN *go back into conversation.)*

DUSZAK: You can't want to hear it *again!*

(Everyone is back to their chitchat, no response. Short pause.)

DUSZAK: But if I must, I must.

EMILY: *(Passing out sausages)* Go ahead, dear. You speak so well.

DUSZAK: Well, I know when my arm is being twisted. Man resists. But man overcomes his resistance. And man grows! So, to begin at the beginning, it was Johnny here who first brought Mr Bal to my attention. Johnny.

JOHNNY: *(Taking a sausage from* EMILY*)* Well, my generator had gone on the whosits. I called the repair shop and Mr Bal was sent to fix it. He arrived late in the afternoon, around five or half past, and as I wrote that night in my journal, my first impression of him was one of, and I quote: "a man who remembers his dreams, a man who knows, and a man who lives."

*(*YOUNG MAN *applauds.)*

ZIEGLER: *(To* YOUNG MAN*)* Shut up, we're not finished with the story yet.

DUSZAK: *(To others, who only casually listen)* You notice how my secretary, Mr Ziegler, says "we" when he means me. How odd to express such participation when only a moment ago he was questioning whether Mr Bal was worthy of such a celebration.

EMILY: *(To* ZIEGLER*)* No!

ZIEGLER: I wasn't saying...

DUSZAK: Of course you weren't saying. You never say. You insinuate. That's all you ever do. That's your type, Ziegler. In this world there are those who insinuate and those who...

ZIEGLER: Who what?

DUSZAK: I forget. *(Grabs his glass)* To Mr Bal!

EVERYONE: *(Stopping their chitchat for a moment to toast)* Mr Bal!

BAL: Is there any mustard?

(PLANTER, *who has returned with the wine, runs out after mustard.)*

DUSZAK: But to continue with our story. Johnny here kept talking about this remarkable young mechanic he had met. In fact, you could say that every third word out of Johnny's mouth was "Bal."

JOHNNY: Bal this. Bal that.

DUSZAK: The "ideas" of Bal. The languages that this Bal knew. The books that this man, Bal, had read.

JOHNNY: I drove you crazy, Mr Duszak.

BAL: *(Eating)* But you couldn't help yourself.

DUSZAK: Johnny drove me crazy. But he kept saying he couldn't help himself.

(ZIEGLER, *a little drunk now, drops a glass, which shatters.)*

DUSZAK: Control yourself, Ziegler. *(Back to the story)* Last week I would have sworn I knew every single educated man left in our district. So you can imagine how incredulous I was. But still one never really knows, does one?

ZIEGLER: Never.

DUSZAK: Man is curious, he questions, he explores! So I felt it almost my duty to meet with this young mechanic, named Bal, and quiz him. And we subsequently met for the first time at Johnny's. And believe me when I say this, but I pulled no punches. I mean, bushes, in my opinion, were not made to be beaten around, if you catch my meaning. So I wanted to know right from the start whether I was wasting my time. So I said to Mr Bal, I said—

JOHNNY: "True hope is swift, and flies with swallow's wings; Kings it makes gods, and meaner creatures kings."

DUSZAK: And Mr Bal, without so much as a breath, replied—what did you reply, Mr Bal?

BAL: *(Reaching for more sausages, with his mouth full)* Richard the Third, Act five, scene two.

DUSZAK: What more is there to say!! To Mr Bal!!

EVERYONE: *(Toasting)* Mr Bal!

(EMILY *gives her husband a kiss as others applaud the end of the story.)*

JOHNNY: *(To* BAL*)* Are you enjoying yourself? You've been terribly quiet. (BAL *knocks over a glass.)* You're not drinking too much, are you, Bal?

BAL: Man eats. Man drinks. Man vomits.

ZIEGLER: *(To a guest, holding his stomach) Excuse me. (Hurries out)*

BAL: Ziegler is a man.

DUSZAK: *(Pushing* JOHNNY *aside)* Excuse me, Johnny. Mr Bal, I just wanted to tell you—before you get the wrong idea, I just wanted to tell you that if it were only up to me, I would, of course, say: "Of course. A man of your talents deserves the top." I would say that, Mr Bal. And I would mean it, too. But it is not up to me.

BAL: *(Trying to stare at* EMILY*)* It's not up to you.

DUSZAK: That's correct. There are other employees, there's seniority, there'd be jealousy. But you're a man of the world, you know how these things work. They take time.

BAL: I know how things work.

DUSZAK: So I will come right to the point then. That's the sort of man I am, Mr Bal. You'll soon learn that working for me.

BAL: I'll learn.

DUSZAK: So here is what I have in mind. I'm thinking—why not bring Mr Bal in as a foreman. A foreman, Mr Bal, it's not the top, but it sure beats being a mechanic. Foreman, I am thinking—foreman...

BAL: And I'm thinking that you are blocking my view.

DUSZAK: What? Oh, of course. This is not the time to talk shop. *(Backs off)* We'll talk later. We'll talk. Don't worry, when I say we'll talk...

BAL: We'll talk.

*(*DUSZAK *moves away;* EMILY *comes by with a tray.)*

PLANTER: *(To* YOUNG WOMAN*)* My uncle once had a barber who spoke ancient Greek.

EMILY: *(To* BAL*)* You're very quiet. I hope we haven't put you off. *(He just stares at her.)* Johnny tells me you might be looking for a new apartment.

BAL: Who isn't?

EMILY: Do you really live in an attic, Mr Bal?

BAL: Is that what Johnny says? *(He drinks.)*

EMILY: He says there rats and awful smells from the street. And he says you never lock your door or close a window. Is that wise, Mr Bal, not to lock your door? *(No response; he stares.)* Johnny says you love fresh air. *(He stares.)* He says you've written books yourself, which you've burned. He says that you told him those books were written only for you. *(He stares.)* He says, Mr Bal is the most fascinating person he has ever met. *(*BAL *holds his head, feeling a bit dizzy.)* My husband owns a few buildings, and I'm sure you could get into one if you'd like.... See, I think about creature comforts. I think a person's surroundings are very important, don't you?... I'm scared of rats myself.... Maybe I should get you some coffee, Mr Bal.

BAL: I would like that. I enjoy watching you walk.

*(*EMILY *leaves.)*

YOUNG MAN: I'll ask him. I'm not afraid to ask him.

PLANTER: Then ask him. No one's stopping you.

YOUNG WOMAN: He is just a mechanic after all.

PLANTER: And he's just been sitting there.

YOUNG WOMAN: If you won't, then I will....

YOUNG MAN: No. I'll do it. I said I'll do it, so I will. *(Goes up to* BAL*)* Mr Bal...

*(*BAL *turns to him.)*

YOUNG MAN: Uh....

YOUNG WOMAN: Mr Bal, we were all wondering, since you have been so... quiet. You have been very, very quiet.

YOUNG MAN: Hardly said a word all night, Mr Bal.

YOUNG WOMAN: Hardly a...

PLANTER: And now that you've had the chance to get to know us...well, we'd sort of like to...

YOUNG MAN: We'd be very interested in...

YOUNG WOMAN: We want to get to know...

ALL THREE: You!

ZIEGLER: *(Who has just returned and heard this)* Speech! Speech!

EVERYONE: Speech! Speech!

(Commotion settles down. Pause. Everyone looks at BAL.*)*

BAL: You want to know what's on my mind? What I'm thinking?

(Everyone nods.)

BAL: I see. Just give me a second or two to collect myself.

(Pause, everyone waits, then finally—)

BAL: I'm thinking—sausages. Good sausages. I'm thinking I wonder when was the last time I had sausages like... But, you know, I can't remember when it was. I'm thinking how I can't remember. I'm thinking, how it must have been a long time ago. *(Short pause)* I'm thinking, on the whole, you are probably pretty decent people. Helpful. Nice. You know. I'm thinking on the other hand that you are also assholes. And I'm thinking I will most probably ridicule you like crazy in the days to come. That sort of thing.... I'm thinking I can't eat another sausage. I'm feeling bloated. I'm thinking how can I use you. A job. An apartment. How can I take advantage. Something along those lines.... What else? Uh, I'm thinking I shouldn't have drunk as much as I have. I feel sort of dizzy. I'm concerned about being sick to my stomach. I'm afraid of embarrassing myself. I'm wondering if I will be constipated in the morning.... I'm thinking—am I speaking out of turn, saying all this? Will they resent me? Then—will I care? And what else?

(EMILY *comes in with the coffee.)*

BAL: Oh yes. There is one more thing. The wife over there. What's your name?

EMILY: *(Confused by the silence of the party)* Emily.

BAL: I am feeling this strong urge to get on top of her. I am. I'm feeling that. And I'm also thinking that I will try to keep her in mind, I will try to think of her, the next time I masturbate.

(Long silence as the lights fade.)

Scene Two (a)

(A rowdy bar. Tables. Noise. JOHNNY, EMILY, *and* JOHANNA *[*JOHNNY*'s young girlfriend] sit at one table.* EMILY *is crying,* JOHNNY *and* JOHANNA *are uncomfortable. At another table,* BAL *is telling a funny story to the* TWO MEN WHO ACT LIKE BEASTS. *They laugh wildly.)*

JOHANNA: Emily, are you okay?

(EMILY *nods, though keeps crying.)*

JOHANNA: *(To* JOHNNY*)* I just don't understand how you could bring me to such a revolting place. I thought I knew you, Johnny, but now I'm beginning to wonder.

JOHNNY: Bal thought we'd enjoy seeing something besides the ends of our own noses, Johanna. He thought we should see the hairs in our noses and the warts on the human face.

JOHANNA: How pretentious! This Mr Bal of yours is just a con man. He's making a fool out of you, Johnny.

JOHNNY: If that's what he's doing, then I'd rather be a fool than a snob. Admit it, maybe you're not enjoying yourself now, but in a day or two you'll be boasting like crazy about having seen all this.

JOHANNA: Five minutes more. That's all. Then I'm going home with or without you.

JOHNNY: Five minutes! Fine. Five minutes to teach you that there's a world beyond your turned-up nose!

(Laughter from BAL *and the* TWO MEN. BAL *wanders over to* EMILY; *he holds an almost empty bottle.)*

BAL: *(To* EMILY*)* Do you have any more cash? This bottle's about had it.

JOHNNY: *(Reaching into his pocket)* Bal, here's some....

*(*BAL *gestures for him to put away his money.* BAL *continues to stare at* EMILY.*)*

EMILY: What were you talking about with those men?

(Pause. BAL *takes her purse.)*

BAL: *(Finally)* You.

(Horse-laughter from the TWO MEN. EMILY *suddenly grabs her purse and hugs it.)*

JOHANNA: *(Standing)* I'm sorry, but I'm leaving....

EMILY: *(To* JOHANNA*)* Please, no!

*(*JOHANNA *stops.)*

BAL: *(To* EMILY*)* You seem to have almost a sexual attachment to that purse. *(To* JOHNNY*)* You know, I once had the same kind of thing with an old brown wallet. Kept patting it. Especially in crowds. Even when I had no money. So it wasn't just that I was patting it to feel secure. I think it was more because the wallet was soft leather. *(Turns back to* EMILY*)* I was telling those two men there what you are like. I mean, your positions; what you moaned. I also told them something else, what was it? Oh right, I remember. I told them how you taste. I let them smell my fingers...

*(*EMILY *cries.)*

JOHANNA: *(To* JOHNNY*)* Stop him!

JOHNNY: Bal...

BAL: Johnny, she asked. She did ask.

EMILY: *(Crying)* You're disgusting!

BAL: That doesn't tell me anything I don't already know. But on the other hand, I'm always fascinated by how other people see me. No matter what they say, that I'm cruel or terrific, doesn't much matter. What I like is that they are talking about me and giving me another point of view from which I can relate to me. That makes me feel in touch with myself.

*(*EMILY *bursts out crying; she tries to hit* BAL, *but he catches her blows. The* TWO MEN *come closer to watch.)*

JOHANNA: *(*JOHNNY *gestures to her for them to leave.)* We can't leave her!

BAL: *(To* EMILY*)* Now look what you've done—you've drawn a crowd. A man stands next to a woman who's sobbing. People will begin to draw conclusions, Emily. And it's the man who will be fingered as the guilty party. And once he begins to feel their hostile stares, he'll want to crawl away and hide. Emily, you've made me feel like I want to crawl away and hide. You have, Emily. *(Screams at her)* You!!!... You've made me feel guilty.

EMILY: I don't know what I ever saw in you!

JOHANNA: He's just sick!

BAL: *(To* JOHANNA*)* Mmmmmm. I too can make judgments of other people. For example, I find her boring. But the moment I make such a judgment, I find myself judging the judgment. Was it "boring" I really meant to say, or was it "tiresome"? That kind of thing.

EMILY: *(Breaks away from* BAL*)* This is a nightmare!

BAL: Now there you have another thing I find people always doing. I see them relating one experience to another—just as you did there with "nightmare" and our situation here—but I wonder if what in fact people really should be doing is trying to precisely articulate for themselves just one experience at a time. Do you see what I mean? But as I'm sure you noticed, I did the very same thing with your purse and my patting my wallet. So who am I to say?

EMILY: Stop him! What are you doing to me?!!!

BAL: What? You don't know? I'm abusing you, Emily. I am being very cruel, even vicious. I am being a bastard. All that is quite clear to me, isn't it to you? *(To* JOHNNY*)* She asked.

*(*EMILY*, crying, moves to leave. The* TWO MEN *suddenly grab her, and attempt to hug and kiss her. She fights and screams.* JOHANNA *screams.* JOHNNY *hesitates, first looking at* BAL*, then at the* TWO MEN*; then he tries to pull them off* EMILY. JOHANNA *helps. She picks up a small chair and tries to hit them.)*

JOHANNA: Get off her! Get the fuck off her!! Fuck you! Fuck you! Fuck you!

(Suddenly, the TWO MEN *stop and simply walk away.* EMILY *cries;* JOHANNA *hugs her;* JOHNNY *breathes heavily.)*

JOHNNY: Bal, why didn't you try to stop that?

BAL: *(Yells)* Because I started that!! Boy, are you thick. Emily's been hanging around my neck for a week, I'm sick of her.... I find that despicable of me, don't you?

JOHANNA: *(Hugging* EMILY*)* She's cut herself. You ought to be ashamed of yourself.

BAL: I am.

JOHANNA: Come. We'll wash it out.

JOHNNY: Bal, what's gotten into you?

BAL: *(Grabs* JOHANNA*'s hand)* Your hands are shaking, are your legs shaking too?

(She pulls away.)

JOHNNY: *(To* JOHANNA*)* He's usually not like this.

EMILY: *(To* JOHANNA*)* He isn't.

JOHANNA: I'm sure.

JOHNNY: It's the whiskey.

JOHANNA: Yes.

EMILY: It is. It's the whiskey.

JOHANNA: Yes.

EMILY: You don't think I'd go with a man who *always* acted like that, do you?

*(*EMILY *and* JOHANNA *leave in the direction of the bathroom.)*

BAL: You're right. It is the whiskey.... And when it's not the whiskey, then it's my upbringing. And when it's not my upbringing, then it's my environment. When it's not my environment, then it's something else. My schooling maybe. Or how about my diet?... Do you have any cash, I want another bottle.

JOHNNY: Bal, I think you've had enough.

BAL: So do I. *(Calls)* Waiter! Another bottle!

Scene Two (b)

(Bathroom of the bar. JOHANNA *looks at the shoulder of* EMILY*'s dress.)*

EMILY: It's ripped, isn't it? It's ruined.

JOHANNA: It's on the seam.

EMILY: It's ripped. He ripped it.

JOHANNA: It's on the seam.

EMILY: I'll never wear it again. I can't.

JOHANNA: Only if you don't want to.

EMILY: I don't. I can't *(Suddenly)* I'm drugged! That's how he got me here. Don't you see? He slipped something into a drink. Who'd have thought. I mean, who would ever have thought. You can't blame me, I'm drugged! *(Turns to* JOHANNA*, no response)* No. But I wish I were. I wish I were something. If not drugged then I wish I had a mental illness. I wish I were out of my senses...

JOHANNA: I have a safety pin in my pocketbook. *(She leaves.)*

EMILY: "I have a safety pin in my pocketbook." Go to hell. *(She tries to see the rip but can't. She takes off her dress, wears only a slip. Looks at the rip.)* It's on the seam.

*(*JOHANNA *returns with her pocketbook, starts to pin the dress.)*

EMILY: So I like sex, so shoot me.

JOHANNA: You don't have to explain.

EMILY: I don't, do I? That's a good one. I'll have to remember that. So I don't have to explain. Just who are you to say that to me?!!! *(She cries, covering her face with her dress. Pause.)*

JOHANNA: Emily? *(No response)* Emily, look, I'll make a little confession of my own.

*(*EMILY *looks up.)*

JOHANNA: I'll bet that if I didn't watch my step, I too could find myself falling for this Mr Bal.

*(*EMILY *looks at her.)*

JOHANNA: See, you shouldn't blame yourself. It could happen to anyone.

EMILY: You're lying, aren't you?

JOHANNA: No.

EMILY: You're just trying to make me feel better, aren't you?

(Pause)

JOHANNA: Yes.

EMILY: You're lying?

JOHANNA: Yes.

EMILY: Good. Bal wouldn't give you the time of day. I'd hate to see you disappointed.

Scene Two (c)

(The bathroom. EMILY, *alone, putting on her makeup.)*

EMILY: Bastard. Son of a bitch. Slime. Shit.

*(*JOHANNA *enters.)*

JOHANNA: Emily?

EMILY: I'm not upset.

JOHANNA: Johnny says if you want to, you could come out now.

EMILY: Nothing happened. Why should I be upset?

JOHANNA: We'll make sure you get home alright. Johnny and me.

EMILY: Rise—that's what I always do. That's how I was brought up. Rise above the stench, hold your nose and lift your head.

JOHANNA: Bal says he is sorry.

EMILY: For what? Nothing happened.

JOHANNA: He's been dancing. He's put on almost a show. He's very funny. Bal is.

EMILY: Rise. *(Stands up)*

JOHANNA: He even tried to get Johnny to get up and dance. But he'd have no part of that.

EMILY: I'm holding my nose. See. That's how I was brought up. *(Leaves)*

JOHANNA: *(After a pause, looks in the mirror)* Whoa. I haven't danced like this in ages. *(Fans herself; stops)* Even my legs are shaking.

Scene Two (d)

(Bathroom. EMILY *and* JOHANNA *enter talking. Both out of breath from dancing.)*

JOHANNA: I think I liked it best when we didn't know who we were supposed to be dancing with. Then I wasn't thinking so much. Then I wasn't trying to be so good at it. I could just sort of let go. *(She giggles.)*

EMILY: Then do. *(Takes off her shoes)* I shouldn't have worn these shoes.

JOHANNA: Do what?

EMILY: Let go. Abandon yourself. Feel the breeze on your cheeks. You're old enough. You told me yourself Johnny's almost begged you.

JOHANNA: He has, but I couldn't. I've thought too much about it. I want to wait until I'm done thinking about it.

EMILY: Flower, woman, flower!

JOHANNA: No.

EMILY: That means yes.

JOHANNA: Maybe.

EMILY: That really means yes. Johnny's not so bad. You'll like it. You'll love it.

JOHANNA: Maybe.

EMILY: You want some advice?

JOHANNA: No.

*(*EMILY *rubs her feet; dance music grows in the background.* JOHANNA *dances, stops.)*

EMILY: *(Looks up at* JOHANNA*, obviously thinking.)* So I like sex...

*(*JOHANNA *turns to* EMILY*.)*

JOHANNA: *(Innocently)* So shoot me.

(They laugh.)

Scene Two (e)

(Bathroom. JOHANNA *alone.)*

JOHANNA: *(To herself)* Mother, Father, close your eyes. And sleep well tonight. I'm grown up. And that can't be helped. *(Recites)*
"Although I joy in thee,
I have no joy of this contract to-night,
It is too rash, too unadvis'd, too sudden,
Too like the lightning, which doth cease to be
Ere one can say it lightens."
How I hated it when Mr Peters made the whole class memorize that.
(Recites) "This bud of love, by summer's ripening breath,
May prove a beauteous flower when next we meet.
Good-night, good-night! as sweet repose and rest
Come to thy heart as that within thy breast!"
(Short pause) Thank you, Mr Peters. Thanks. *(Leaves, calling)* Johnny! Johnny!

Scene Three (a)

*(*BAL*'s attic. Bed.* JOHANNA *in bed, covering herself with the covers.*
BAL *sits on the edge of the bed.)*

JOHANNA: I don't believe what I've done. How did this happen?

BAL: First, I unbuttoned your blouse, then I stuck your hand inside my pants.... *(*JOHANNA *covers her ears.)* You asked me a question.

JOHANNA: I'm confused. This room. I don't even know where I am.

BAL: You can start by blaming your sweetheart, Johnny. If that boy could hold his liquor, he wouldn't have passed out and left me to take you home.

JOHANNA: Then why didn't you?! Why didn't you just take me home?!!

BAL: It must have been the whiskey.

JOHANNA: They'll notice. Everyone will notice. I can't go back there. I can't. *(Quickly turns to* BAL*)* Bal, I love you. Let's go away, Bal. Dear, come. I'll write home. After we're settled, my parents can come and visit. They'll see I did the right thing. I'll show them. They'll forgive and forget. Where's my blouse? *(Hysterical)* Where's my blouse?!!!

*(*BAL *has been sitting on it. He hands it to her.)*

JOHANNA: Well—pack! What are you waiting for? Pack!!!!

BAL: The only place I'm going is into the bathroom. I want to wash myself.

JOHANNA: What?!! You have to go with me! *(Short pause)* I want that!!! *(She collapses; to herself.)* God, what was I thinking of. Go away with... I'd sooner die. I'd sooner slit my wrists. No one will know. I don't look so different. Do I? Do I?!! And who's going to find out? I'm not going to tell anybody. I'm not going to tell a soul. And you won't either, will you? *(Short pause)* Will you?!!!

BAL: I never know what I'm going to do. Only what I've already done, Johanna.

JOHANNA: Promise me!!! *(No response)* Promise me!!!!!!

BAL: As a matter of fact, knowing me as I do, once I see my best friend Johnny's face, I'm probably not going to be able to resist telling. Just out of curiosity, I suppose. To see his reaction. I wish I could promise, Johanna. I really wish I could. No, that's not true. I'm past the point of wishing. I never wish, anymore. Do you want to hear something funny? I hate wishing wells. I do. I detest them. I find them loathsome. It's true. There's something I'll bet you didn't know about me. *(Pause)* I'm not a very good person, Johanna.

JOHANNA: *(Hysterical, screams)* Noooooooooooooo!!!!!!! *(She runs out. Long pause.)*

BAL: *(Sincerely, to himself)* I feel very guilty.

Scene Three (b)

(The attic. BAL *and the* CRAP-PLAYER *have just finished a game of craps.)*

CRAP-PLAYER: *(At the window)* They're still dredging the river for that poor girl.

BAL: *(Counting out money)* Johanna.

CRAP-PLAYER: So you did know her.

BAL: Who told you I did? *(No response)* I knew her boyfriend. *(Handing him the money)* Here's eighty, I'll give you the rest on Friday. You don't have to count it.

CRAP-PLAYER: *(Counting the money)* My landlady saw her jump. That was fortunate.

BAL: Because she called the police?

CRAP-PLAYER: No, because now she has something besides me to talk about. One more game?

(BAL shakes his head, gets a cigarette.)

CRAP-PLAYER: Just want to give you a fair shake. Never know when your luck will turn.

BAL: No such animal as luck.

CRAP-PLAYER: No?

BAL: No. If I roll a poor game, there are reasons.

CRAP-PLAYER: Are there?

BAL: Reasons because I chose not to shake one more time or one less time. Reasons why I threw hard or not so hard. Reasons for my hands being sweaty—or dry. Reasons. I may be tense. I might be preoccupied. I may be uncomfortable in this shirt—the sleeve might be too tight. Luck's got shit to do with anything. There are reasons.

CRAP-PLAYER: If you say so, Bal. *(He starts to leave, stops again at the window. They both look out now. Pause.)*

BAL: Women seem more prone to suicide than men. Maybe it has something to do with hormones.

Scene Four (a)

(River bank. Park bench. JOHNNY sits on the bench, MAN WITH A FISHING POLE fishes.)

MAN WITH A FISHING POLE: *(To the fish)* Come on, fishies. Come on now. You're trying my patience. Yum-yum fishies. Yum-yum.... *(Pause. He fishes. Then to JOHNNY:)* I've never seen it like this. Two hours and not a bite. You don't happen to have a match, do you?

(JOHNNY gives him a match. MAN lights it.)

MAN WITH A FISHING POLE: This is a trick I thought up myself. Burn half of the worm. They like that. Fish are getting more sophisticated every day. Well-done, medium rare. They have their tastes like you or I. Just got to find out what it is, and you got them. *(Fishes)* I give 'em a few more years before they start asking for ketchup and English muffins. Come on now, don't we have any well-done worm lovers in this crowd? *(Pauses; fishes)* Come on fishies. It's chow-time. Soup's on, fishies. I said, soup's on. *(Fishes)* Nothing. Well, I guess I can't blame 'em, I mean I wouldn't bite on no worm, if it is cooked to taste, when I had a whole young girl down there to chew on.

VOICE OFF: They've found her!!!

*(*MAN WITH A FISHING POLE *quickly collects his things and starts to hurry off.)*

MAN WITH A FISHING POLE: *(To* JOHNNY*)* You better hurry, fella, if you want to see. They'll be covering her up once they get her on dry ground. *(He runs out.)*

(Pause. JOHNNY *starts to get up, stops. Pause. Suddenly and violently he turns against the bench and begins kicking and hitting it. Boards are broken. He smashes these boards, too, against the bench until finally the bench is a pile of rubble.* JOHNNY *pants. Pause.)*

JOHNNY: *(To himself)* I had to get that out.

Scene Four (b)

(A confessional. Church bells ring. BAL *kneels before a closed curtain. He is sobbing.)*

BAL: *(After a pause)* See, now that's just my point, Father. Do you see? Here I am sobbing. I can't help myself. But the point is not that I can't help myself, but it's the phrase itself—"I am sobbing." Or, rather, it's the idea that I am sobbing, not the phrase. After all, I don't want to make this a linguistic problem. It's the idea that is so terrifyingly inappropriate, or, better, so horrendously untrue. Take my feet, Father. Are *they* sobbing? Can they sob? Or my hair. Or my elbow. What have *they* got to do with sobbing? Have you ever heard the expression— "The sum of all parts"? I am the sum of my parts, Father, so then how can I sob? My eyes, they tear. My throat, it dries. So, then, who or what is doing all this sobbing? *(Short pause)* Not me. It's definitely not me. Each part's too goddamn busy touching the next—like cogs, you see. Like electrical wires. They're much too busy to sob. Oh, I know what you're going to say—I know your argument. You're going to say—if I were to whack a finger off, would that finger still be me? Would that bloody finger over there in the garbage be me? And you'd say, of course it wouldn't. It's not the finger, you'd say, it is the pain. It is what you are feeling which is you. Which is me. But, Father, the pain would only be in here. In here. *(Points to his head)* Just here. Not in my foot. Not in the back of my neck. Only here. So it always comes back to what's in here, does it? *(Pause)* But, Father, I am more than a brain. There's more. There is! I am not just a goddamn brain!!! *(He sobs. Pause. He relaxes.)*

*(*PRIEST *enters from the side, holding a small paper bag.)*

PRIEST: Can I help, son?

BAL: *(Standing)* Done. I got it out.

PRIEST: But...?

BAL: I said, I got it out.

*(*BAL *leaves.* PRIEST *opens the curtain, there is no one there. He takes a cup of coffee out of the bag, opens the lid, sips.)*

PRIEST: Next! *(Closes the curtain)*

Scene Five (a)

*(*BAL*'s attic.* JOHNNY, *alone, sits in a chair, waiting. He hears steps and hides.* BAL *enters with* SOPHIE, *who is in her twenties.)*

SOPHIE: Hey, let go! Let go of my arm!

*(*BAL *lets go.)*

SOPHIE: I don't even know who you are. *(Looks around)* Jesus, is this where you live? What are you, a criminal or something? *(Turns back to* BAL*)* Hey, what makes you think you can just snatch a girl off the street and drag her off to your filthy room?

BAL: You weren't dragged. You walked.

SOPHIE: So I walked. What's that supposed to mean? I was afraid you'd hit me.

BAL: Oh. *(He opens the door so she can leave.)*

SOPHIE: What are you doing? You telling me to leave? What are you, sick? You drag me off the street and up God knows how many steps to this rat's nest just to tell me to leave? I'll leave when I'm ready to leave. I have to catch my breath.

BAL: Oh. *(He closes the door again.)*

SOPHIE: If I'm not home by nine they'll lock me out.

BAL: There's your incentive to hurry.

SOPHIE: If my mother found out she'd throw me out. My own mother would. I hate her. What's your name?

BAL: Bal.

SOPHIE: That's a stupid name. Mine's Sophie and that's a stupid name too. My grandmother was Sophie too and she was even stupider than her name. What do you do?

BAL: Eat.

SOPHIE: Oh, that's clever. A man who not only lives in a hole in the wall but is clever besides. Boy, this is my lucky day. You want to know what I do?

BAL: No.

SOPHIE: Hey, you've got a great line, you know that? You're a real charmer.

(BAL *tries to kiss her.)*

SOPHIE: Stop that! Haven't you ever heard about conversation? It's when two people talk. One after the other. See, first you talk, then I talk. Or first I talk, then you talk. I'm flexible.

(BAL *tries to kiss her again.)*

SOPHIE: Hold it, will you?

(BAL *backs away.)*

SOPHIE: Brother, how long you been in this closet, a million years?... Now, so you want to know what I do, do you, well, I'll tell you....

BAL: *(Screams)* Look!!! *(Calm)* Try for a minute to understand my side of this, okay? I am trying very hard to forget someone. As you may know, there are many ways one can go about accomplishing this. Alcohol is but one. Drugs another. And a third and possibly the best way to forget someone you have had sex with is to find someone else to have sex with. To get that someone else's smell on my body. That sort of thing. I could be more poetic if you want, but I am tired. So that is what I am trying to accomplish, and if it's not going to be you, then I would like to know now while there's still enough time tonight to dig up someone else.

(JOHNNY *comes out of hiding.* SOPHIE *reacts in shock and surprise.)*

BAL: Johnny. *(Pause)*

JOHNNY: Bal. *(Short pause)* Bal, don't you ever make your bed? Or... change your sheets? I'm not a fanatic or anything, but that's just the kind of thing that would drive me mad. If it were my bed, I mean.... You want me to get some clean sheets? Be no trouble. God, you must have had them on since... for weeks. *(Pause)* It's really a shame about—you know. I mean if I've said it once I've said it a thousand times, someday someone's going to fall into that river. That bank's pretty damn steep.... Not all that steep, but steep. And the current... I've said it a thousand times. *(Pause)* But who knows, you know. A lot of possible things could have happened to.... Anything could have happened. Right? There are a thousand possibilities. *(Pause)* Aren't there? *(Pause)*

BAL: Uh. *(Thinks)* No, I don't think so.

*(*JOHNNY *makes a slight groan. Long pause)*

BAL: You know, I've been thinking about you. I know at the moment it may not look like it, but I have. I've been thinking a whole lot about you, Johnny. I've been thinking... *(Begins to count out his thoughts)* how very sorry I am—not only for Johanna, but also for you. I've been thinking what a jerk you were for letting your girl get to know me. I've been thinking that because you never got the chance yourself, that I've wanted to tell you that Johanna, she was, Johnny, quite a spirited lover. Very lively and instinctual. *(Short pause)* I've been thinking a lot of things, Johnny, but some of those thoughts have been about *you. (Pause)* I wanted you to know that. It might help to know that you've been on my mind. *(Pause)*

JOHNNY: I'm peeing. *(Short pause. To* SOPHIE.*)* Excuse me, I can't help it. *(His pants are wet.)*

Scene Five (b)

(The attic. BAL *and* SOPHIE *in bed.* JOHNNY *sits at a distance with his head down. In the dark,* BAL *screams.)*

SOPHIE: You scared me half to death.

BAL: *(Turning on a light)* I had a nightmare. *(He sits up.)* Hand me that notepad.

(She does and goes back to sleep. To JOHNNY.*)*

BAL: I have to write down my nightmare before I forget it. *(Writes)* Whenever I have a dream such as I just did, I find I am compelled to get as much as I can down on paper. I take it as almost an obligation. As if my brain were sending signals and clues about me, Bal. *(Writes)* The real trick is to try not to structure the dream. Just get it all down as I remember it. But, of course, some structuring is bound to happen; but that itself can be significant, because what one remembers can tell you as much about yourself as the dream itself can. Maybe more. *(Writes)* There are days when I do nothing but read through years of my dreams. It's after one of those days that I feel that my two feet are firmly planted on the ground. *(Finishes. To* SOPHIE*)* Roll over. Your breath smells.

(She rolls over. To JOHNNY*)*

BAL: What are you doing, Johnny?

JOHNNY: Praying.

BAL: Mankind is so resilient. And that warms my heart. *(Short pause)* But not my feet. *(To* SOPHIE*)* Quit stealing the covers, will you?
(He pulls covers over him and continues to read through his dreams.)

Scene Six (a)

(A garage. BAL *fiddles with a generator;* JOHNNY *sits and watches;* BOSS *is screaming at an unseen customer.)*

BOSS: So take your lousy generator and shove it!!! You think I care?! You think you're breaking my heart?!! Oh, it's breaking. My heart is breaking. Ouch! Ouch! I said get the hell out of my garage! I don't need any business from an asshole! *(Turns to* BAL *and* JOHNNY*)* Did you hear me? I don't need business from any asshole. Who the hell does that man think I am? What am I, his lackey? Just because he's in a shitty mood, just because he's got a hag for a wife—oh I've seen her. Thank God I was wearing my sunglasses! *(Turns back)* Don't dump on me, fella!! *(Back to* BAL *and* JOHNNY*)* Tell me something, do I look like a shrink? Do I look like I work in a hospital? Then why are so many of my customers mentally sick?!! Tell me that, will you? Will somebody please explain that to me?!! Oh Christ. *(Calms down. Points at* BAL*'s generator.)* So what's wrong with that one?

BAL: It's broken.

BOSS: Oh, that's clever, that's very informative. Maybe I should restate my question—what is broken, Mr Bal?

BAL: The casing is cracked. Cracked casing, no vacuum, no vacuum, no pressure, no pressure, no movement, no movement, it's broken.

BOSS: Cute. Very cute. Can you fix it?

*(*BAL *looks over the generator.)*

BOSS: I said, can you fix it? Is it fixable?! Watch my lips!

BAL: Have to seal the casing.

BOSS: Good, then do it.

*(*BAL *stands, staring at the* BOSS.*)*

BOSS: What are you doing? I said, do it.

*(*BAL *stares.)*

BOSS: Oh Christ, I said fix it!

*(*BAL *doesn't move.)*

BOSS: Look, I'm not in the mood to take any shit from a punk. I don't need shit from a punk. Do you understand me, punk? *(Pushes him)* Do you, punk?

Punk. Punk. Get the hell out of here and don't come back. You make me sick to my stomach. *(Starts to leave, turns to* JOHNNY*)* I don't need any shit from an asshole!

(He leaves. JOHNNY *looks at* BAL. *Pause.* BAL *sits down with the generator. Throughout the beginning of the next speech,* BAL *repairs the generator, sealing the casing with tape, etc.)*

BAL: So I'm fired. I'm out of work. If I'm out of work I'll go on the dole. I'll become part of the idle poor. My dole will come out of the pockets of the middle class, who will then grow to resent me. I will have no incentive to work, because I'll be paid not to work. I'll wear tennis shoes and carry radios and stand on streetcorners. Programs will be set up to help me, which the rest of society will pay for and resent. Then they will lose *their* incentive. More people on the dole, less work. Prices will rise. Governments will get bigger. Maybe I'll get into trouble with the law. Money will be spent to keep me in jail, then to keep me out of jail. I will eat other people's money. I will be an open wound, a gaping hole that devours money.... *(He has fixed the generator. He now turns it on—it works. He turns it off. Throughout the rest of the speech, he takes the generator apart, piece by piece.)* On the other hand, maybe I'm the type who will pull himself up by his bootstraps. I will forge ahead. Maybe I'll bounce into a new position and turn this once bad break to my advantage. Maybe something great and wonderful will come along and I will learn to feel superior to all the shmucks I've surpassed. And I will grow to resent every lazy bugger who has his hand in my pocket or stuck in my face. And I will learn to project my face into theirs and refrain: "I did it, why can't they?" And I will breathe disgust but appear to give handouts gladly, because gladly I will want to keep them in their place. While at the same time voting against all social programs—not out of spite, but as an act of education, because I will want it shown just whose hand has been feeding whom.

Or maybe I will become a liberal thinker and drop phrases like "fairness" and "equal protection" as if I were a pigeon dropping my shit, while at the same time I send my kids off to private school and while at the same time I keep an eye on their Puerto Rican mammy, making sure she does not get the rickets. Or the silver.

Or maybe I'll be a good old boy and simply flail frustrated and angry and call a nigger a nigger, a spade a spade, and a bottle of beer mother's milk. Or maybe I'll become a communist. Or a socialist. Or a socialist with communist leanings, or a social democrat, or a populist conservative Democrat, or a conservative populist Democrat with Republican sympathies, or a Fascist, or a neo-Fascist conservative, or simply a Fascist communist.

Whatever. There are many possibilities, aren't there? And we'll just have to wait and see what kind of man I am. I don't know about you, Johnny, but the future intrigues me—and I can't wait to watch. *(The generator is in pieces. He stands, kicks over the generator.)* See, I know how these things work.

Scene Six (b)

(A road on the way out of town. BAL *and* JOHNNY *sit on the edge of the road. Evening.* BAL *now has a very large radio, which is playing very loud dance music. He wears tennis shoes, which are unlaced.* BAL *is eating a sandwich. He looks at* JOHNNY, *offers him half of the sandwich,* JOHNNY *shakes his head.* BAL *turns down the radio.)*

BAL: Eat. Then digest. Then shit. Then fertilize. Then grow. Then pick. Then eat. We have to eat, Johnny. We have an obligation to eat. *(Turns up the radio, then turns it down again)* Johnny, have you ever had that urge to startle yourself? You know, to do something, then after you've done it, you're surprised that you did it. It's not easy, is it? *(Short pause. He belches.)* Nope, I knew that was coming. *(Pause. Suddenly slaps himself in the face)* Nah, I wasn't surprised. But I'm sort of surprised how much that hurt. I wonder if that counts. No. *(Short pause)* Wait, I have an idea. *(He stands.)* First I have to think of something else—so my mind's preoccupied. What should I think about, Johnny? Wait, I got it. *(Recites)* "Shall I compare thee to a summer's day...?" *(He suddenly throws his feet out from under himself and falls.)* No. I caught myself with my shoulder, so I must have known that was coming. I'll try it again. *(Stands)* Where was I? *(Recites)* "Shall I compare thee to a summer's day? Thou art more lovely and more temperate. Rough winds do... something to the something buds of May. And something something something." I can't remember it. That sort of surprises me. *(He suddenly throws his feet out from under himself again and falls.)* Nope. The shoulder again. God damn it. This is difficult, Johnny.

JOHNNY: Bal...?

BAL: *(Getting up)* Johnny, do me a favor, will you, and divert me for a moment. Come on, divert me. Maybe if my mind's occupied with something you do, I'll be able to startle me.

JOHNNY: Bal, I know what you've done.

BAL: So do I. *(Suddenly turns to his side and yells)* There's Johanna! Look!!!

*(*JOHNNY *looks.)*

BAL: God damn it!!! That startled you, but not me. Well, anyway, thanks for trying. Thanks for trying to divert me. *(He sits and takes out the sandwich again.)* You know, I really don't know if maybe I'm just a complete jerk. I haven't decided yet. *(Pause)* Johnny, have you ever thought ahead? I mean, have you ever thought not about what you were doing, but what you were about to do? And if what you were about to do, you did, have you ever thought about what you would do then? And then? Have you ever thought so far ahead that you forgot that you were breathing? Have you? I'm asking you, Johnny. I'm very interested in what other people have to say—it gives me time to catch my breath, before we get back to talking about me.

JOHNNY: Bal...

BAL: *(Interrupting)* On my more confident days, I feel like I am the most fascinating person alive. On my more lethargic days, I am the laziest man there ever was. When I'm thirsty, I'm as parched as a desert. When I piss, it terrifies me to think that there are other toilets flushing clear across the earth.

JOHNNY: Bal, I want to talk.

BAL: I thought we were.

*(*JOHNNY *looks away.)*

BAL: Ah! I see. When you say "talk," I'll bet what you really mean is "argue." I understand. What you in fact mean, Johnny, is that you wish me to commit myself to some phrase or some line of thought, so you can cut me off in mid-stride and twist and distort what may have only been meant to be an offhand remark into something I must now defend with my life, for my self-respect. I see.

You want to take the aggressor's role and leave me the defender's. You want to jab away and pick at my words as if they were the last pieces of flesh on a white bone.

And all you'll need is that one phrase out of my mouth and you'll think you've got me pegged and cornered, and me, like a trapped mouse, I'll be too afraid to breathe, too afraid to utter shit, because I'll see you there, set to pounce and criticize and humiliate and abuse, set to make me feel not only less than you—less witty or less eloquent— but also make me feel less a man than I think I am. Fine.

Well, let's try it. Try me. I'm game. Go ahead and answer me. Answer me!!!

JOHNNY: Bal...!

BAL: *(Screaming)* Answer me! Debate! Debate! Debate! *(Suddenly jumping up and down)* I win! I win! I win!

*(*JOHNNY *turns away.* BAL *shrugs, turns the radio back up.)*

BAL: *(Moving to the music)* I'd love to be dancing right now. *(Short pause)* Actually, it's not so much the dancing that I want, as it is the sweating. I'd love to be sweating right now.

Scene Seven (a)

(The edge of the woods. BAL *and* JOHNNY *have stopped walking.* SOPHIE *is a short distance from them.)*

JOHNNY: She must have gone out of her mind trying to find us.

SOPHIE: So?

BAL: She's desperate.

SOPHIE: It wasn't so hard. Really.

JOHNNY: She looks exhausted, doesn't she?

SOPHIE: I'll be all right. Don't worry.

BAL: *(To* JOHNNY*)* And whenever I see someone who is desperate, I immediately think—"fair game." I wonder why that is. *(Pause)*

SOPHIE: You know, you can just tell me to go. You can. *(Pause)* I don't care.... I mean, who cares? *(Silence. To* BAL*)* My mother locked me out.

JOHNNY: I'm sorry.

SOPHIE: *(To* JOHNNY*)* Fuck off! *(Pause. To* BAL*)* She wouldn't even come to the door.... Yeh, and I'm pounding 'til my knuckles start bleeding. And then, see, she sticks her stupid head out the window and starts screaming—"Slut! Slut!"

JOHNNY: Bal...?

SOPHIE: *(Screams)* Leave him alone, he's listening to me!!! *(Pause. She tries to smile but is close to tears. To* BAL.*)* My legs were shaking.

(He looks at her.)

SOPHIE: I was out there all alone on the street, see, and then like these other heads, you know, they're popping out of other windows. And they're shouting. Some of 'em are even spitting down at me. My mother's yelling to everyone how I hadn't come home that night and how she, you know, didn't have a daughter. It was kind of like being a kid again. Looking up at everybody. You know that feeling? So I start running off and then I fall and cut myself and they're laughing and me, wouldn't you know it, me I'm just trying to be dignified. *(Crying now, but trying not to show it. Pause.)* Bal, I really love you. I do love you, Bal.

BAL: I heard you the first time. *(To* JOHNNY*)* Whenever I hear someone repeating themselves, I immediately think—"desperate." *(Pause)*

SOPHIE: *(Very awkward and self-conscious now)* You want me to go, I'll go. I'll understand. I must look a mess. *(Pause)* Look, who's begging? I'm not begging. *(Silence)*

JOHNNY: *(Quietly)* How long ago was this?

SOPHIE: *(Shaking)* Do you know what today is?

JOHNNY: *(Shrugs)* Saturday?

SOPHIE: *(Shrugs)* Maybe a week ago. Maybe.

JOHNNY: And since then?

SOPHIE: Bal, I want to be with you!

BAL: If you stay, I'll hurt you. I'll mistreat you. You'll end up despising me.

SOPHIE: I don't believe that.

BAL: *(Yells)* It's true!!! *(Pause. Calmly)* Look, I know me.

Scene Seven (b)

(The woods. Gray. Nearly winter. JOHNNY *and* SOPHIE *stand together watching the sky.* BAL, *at a distance, stands over what we learn is a corpse. Pause.)*

JOHNNY: Gray. Going to snow.

SOPHIE: *(Nods)* You can feel it.

JOHNNY: You can. In your bones.

SOPHIE: No. *(Pause)* For me it's the shoulders. I always feel it first in my shoulders. I have sensitive shoulders.

JOHNNY: Huh. For me, it's my bones.

(Pause. They watch the sky.)

SOPHIE: Makes me feel like I'm on a ship.

JOHNNY: What does?

SOPHIE: The snow coming. Like I'm standing on a ship and way over there on the horizon, across the sea, it's coming. And I'm bobbing up and down—watching, leaning on a rail. Of course, I've never been on a ship, but it makes me feel like I'm on one. *(Pause)* It's coming. *(Long pause)*

JOHNNY:
"When all aloud the wind doth blow,
And coughing drowns the parson's saw,
And birds sit brooding in the snow,
And Marion's nose looks red and raw;
When roasted crabs hiss in the bowl,
Then nightly sings the staring owl,
'Tu-whit, tu-who!'—
A merry note."

SOPHIE: What's that? Something you made up?

JOHNNY: *(Shakes his head)* Something I know.

(They move toward BAL.*)*

BAL: *(Over the corpse)* Dust to dust. Rotten flesh to rotten flesh. His eyes are closed. He must have known what was happening to him. Starvation, I would guess.

JOHNNY: *(Retches)* Jesus!

SOPHIE: Bal, can we go?

BAL: Once I asked a doctor what exactly takes place when a body dies. He told me that dead bodies were none of his business. I've been meaning to ask an undertaker ever since. But what I've been able to surmise or what I remember of what I once surmised, from the light reading I had done on the subject, is that more often than not, the heart goes first, then the blood stops flowing, the brain fails once it has used the blood that remained in the brain, then the veins become quickly limp then just as quickly tight, and they stretch and then they crack. The flesh then soaks up what remains of the body's fluids; so the product then is not unlike a marsh, that is where on the surface there are solids, but underneath there is only soft mud.

SOPHIE: Bal, really, it makes me sick.

BAL: That, Sophie, is due totally to your upbringing. Death has been hidden from us, so it frightens us and makes us ill. Actually, a body like this cannot harm you, Sophie. Your fear is all in your head.... Go ahead and touch it.

JOHNNY: Bal!

BAL: Go ahead, Sophie, it won't bite.

SOPHIE: *(Hesitating)* But I...

BAL: Forget it. *(Starts to leave)*

SOPHIE: No, Bal, wait! *(She touches it.)* It's spongy.

JOHNNY: Why do you listen to him?

BAL: See, it didn't jump up and eat you.... Now kiss it. Come on, on the mouth.

JOHNNY: Bal, how can you ask her to do that?

*(*BAL *shrugs.)*

SOPHIE: Kiss it? Oh, I can't, Bal. Really I...

BAL: *(Moves to leave)* Suit yourself.

SOPHIE: Wait, Bal!

*(*BAL *stops. She bends down and kisses the corpse.)*

SOPHIE: Worms!

(She chokes. Pause. They start to leave.)

JOHNNY: Bal, aren't you going to touch it?

BAL: Me? *(Pause)* No. No, corpses give me the willies.

Scene Seven (c)

(A hut. BAL *and* JOHNNY *sit at a table drinking.* SOPHIE *sits on a bed, sobbing. She is slowly taking off her clothes, getting ready for bed. Pause.)*

BAL: *(To* JOHNNY*)* Excuse me. *(He walks over to* SOPHIE.*)* You're crying. You're upset. You're feeling terrible. Eyes bloodshot. Hands pale. You're trembling. You have regrets. Regret after regret. You have a tear that has crawled all the way to your chin. *(He moves away, turns back.)* It helps to know how you are. *(Returns to the table)*

*(*SOPHIE *continues to sob, though very quietly now. Long pause)*

JOHNNY: Why don't I leave? Was that the question?

BAL: Yes. *(Silence)*

JOHNNY: The way you abuse that woman makes me sick to my stomach.

BAL: Is that just a way of speaking, or is your reaction really so physical?

*(*JOHNNY *looks away.)*

BAL: Just curious. *(Silence)* Johanna.

*(*JOHNNY *looks back at him.)*

BAL:Did I say something wrong? Can I help it if when I look at you I think of her? If I see your eyes and remember hers? That's how my mind works. Can I help that? *(He puts his head on the table and cries.)* The problem with tears is that they are difficult to read. Even from the inside. Once I thought I was very sad, but I only had a speck of dust on my pupil. I've had a similar experience with a lump in my throat. Whenever I now feel a lump in my throat, I immediately think—"chicken bone." *(Pours drinks for himself and* JOHNNY.*)*

(Silence)

JOHNNY: *(A little drunk)* What you said about the lump in your throat and the chicken bone made me think about a certain park bench. I shattered this bench with my own hands. When I was through I felt a lot better. I felt better because my hand hurt now. The pain was there. I could see it. *(Suddenly, he takes out a notepad and writes furiously; finishes.)*

BAL: *(Takes what* JOHNNY *has just written and reads)* "Sunday in January. Bal cries. He talks of sadness. All I want to do is slit his throat. I want to take a broken bottle—a green broken bottle, or a red one with two jagged edges, and I want to hold it right next to his throat and I want to watch his eyes. I want that. I want to slit that throat. The throat. His..." *(To* JOHNNY*)* What's this word?

JOHNNY: *(Looks at the notepad)* "Throat."

BAL: "His throat. His throat. Please." *(Pause. He hands back the notepad.)* It helps to get upset every once in a while.

*(*SOPHIE *cries.* JOHNNY *is almost frozen.* BAL *stands, looks at one and then the other, and puts out one hand for each of them.)*

BAL: *(Proud)* We're a very emotional group. We are. *(Smiles)*

Scene Seven (d)

(The hut. BAL *and* JOHNNY *at the table, as before.* SOPHIE *is asleep in bed. Pause.* JOHNNY *stands and begins to strip down to his shorts. He sits back down.)*

JOHNNY: Hot.

*(*BAL *nods. Pause.)*

BAL: *(Points to the bed)* You want to get in?

JOHNNY: What are you, a pimp?

BAL: You don't want to fuck her?

JOHNNY: You're disgusting. She's in love with you.

BAL: Her mother wouldn't let her back in, she had nowhere to go, she felt like the world had closed in on her, she'd run out of options, she ran into us, "an option," she told herself, so she fell in love.

JOHNNY: Is that what you think?

BAL: That's what I think, whether it's true or not. But it is what I think and that is what matters, doesn't it?

(Pause. BAL *goes to the bed, picks up the covers and shows* SOPHIE*, who is naked, to* JOHNNY.*)*

JOHNNY: Bal, what do you want?

BAL: I want to entice you into bed with her. I've got it into my head that the sight of you two in a good healthy clinch would be pleasing to me. Though at the same time, I am feeling rather guilty at the thought. I'm wondering—is that a sick thought? Does this show me up as having certain perverse inclinations? And then I'm thinking—but it's society that dictates what is and is not perverse. And then I'm thinking—but I am part of society. And then I'm thinking—I am what I am.

JOHNNY: Go to hell.

(JOHNNY *turns away.* BAL *shrugs and goes back to the table. Pause.)*

BAL: Isn't there anything I can do for you? Something? There must be. You just have to let me know, Johnny. You just have to let me help. I want to offer my help.

JOHNNY: Why?

BAL: I enjoy the feeling.

JOHNNY: Ah. *(Short pause)*

BAL: Once I saw a child screaming in the street. He came up to me and asked me to take him home, to his mother. I said, sure, kid. I said— sure.

JOHNNY: And?

BAL: And then I left him. I felt terrific. What more could I do? I offered. Isn't that enough? I'm offering, Johnny, isn't that enough?

(SOPHIE *wakes up, gets out of bed—naked.)*

SOPHIE: I'm going to get myself a beer. Anyone want one?

(They don't respond; she shrugs and exits.)

BAL: *(To* JOHNNY*)* Hot?

Scene Seven (e)

(The hut. Night. SOPHIE *and* JOHNNY *in bed, asleep in each other's arms.* BAL *enters. He suddenly rips the covers off them. They shriek.)*

BAL: Peek-a-boo!

(He laughs and giggles with childish pleasure. SOPHIE *and* JOHNNY *just stare at him.)*

SOPHIE: *(Coldly, to* JOHNNY*)* He's drunk.

(They cover themselves up. Pause.)

BAL: *(Quietly)* Yes. *(Short pause)* Everything is chemical.

Scene Seven (f)

(A clearing near a pond. SOPHIE *and* JOHNNY *have just run in, out of breath, though smiling. They have been swimming and are naked.* BAL *sits at a distance.)*

JOHNNY: *(Toweling himself)* One more dip?

SOPHIE: Hand me my blouse.

JOHNNY: It's not cold. It's rather refreshing. I feel refreshed.

(She takes her blouse.)

JOHNNY: Don't you?

(SOPHIE giggles.)

JOHNNY: No?

(She giggles again.)

JOHNNY: Might be the last pond for days.

SOPHIE: Might.

JOHNNY: Best make the best of it. You look refreshed.

(SOPHIE giggles again)

JOHNNY: You do. I'll go myself then. *(Smiling, he slaps her fanny with the towel.)* I will. *(He does it again.)*

SOPHIE: *(Laughing, slaps him back—all very playful)* No you won't. Nope.

JOHNNY: *(Continuing)* Here I go! I'm going!

(They stop and just stand and laugh. SOPHIE suddenly becomes quiet.)

SOPHIE: *(With a faint smile)* One more dip. *(She begins to take her blouse off.)*

BAL: *(Calmly)* You two are disgusting.

(SOPHIE and JOHNNY stop and turn to him.)

BAL: You are. They way you act. You take off your clothes right in front of me. Paw each other. Prance around. You're shameless. You're disgusting.... I don't mean that as a criticism. I'm not saying that's either good or bad. All I'm saying is that that is what is generally meant by the word "disgusting." Isn't it? *(Slowly they begin to put their clothes on.)* I mean, you two fit the definition. I'm not saying this against you. I don't mean that. Don't misunderstand me.... What's wrong? What did I do?

(SOPHIE and JOHNNY are very somber.)

BAL: Hey, doesn't anyone want to talk ideas anymore???

Scene Eight (a)

(Plain. Wind. BAL enters. He holds his hair back and sticks his face into the wind.)

BAL: Ahhh. Listen to that wind. *(Makes wind noise)* Mmmmmmm. Feel it. Ahhh. *(Makes wind noise. Softly.)* Blow. Blow. Blow. Yes. Ahhhhh. *(Laughs with great pleasure)*

(JOHNNY enters. He is cold.)

JOHNNY: *(Shivering)* Shit.

BAL: Have we lost her?

JOHNNY: You'd like that, wouldn't you?

BAL: I don't know what I'd like. At the moment my mind's pretty much blank. If anything, I guess you could say I'm concentrating on walking, though there is a little tune that keeps running through my mind. *(Starts to leave, stops; to* JOHNNY*)* Do you hear it? *(He exits.)*

JOHNNY: *(Calls)* Sophie! Sophie!

(He runs out. Pause. JOHNNY *reenters with* SOPHIE, *who is pregnant now.)*

SOPHIE: *(Entering)* That's a hard question for me to answer, Johnny. I'm not sure why I won't go off with you. You'd make a hell of a better father than Bal ever would. You'd be reliable. I could trust you. But I just have this fixed idea in my head that Bal is the man for me. And I can't let go of the thought. I just can't help myself. *(She starts to leave.)*

JOHNNY: *(Quietly)* Sophie?

(She stops; they stare at each other.)

SOPHIE: Johnny, *you* see someone in trouble and you just have to help. You're one of those kind. You are. *(She turns to leave.)*

JOHNNY: Sophie!!

(She stops.)

JOHNNY: Sophie, I just want you to know—Jesus Christ, I can't believe I'm going to say this—

SOPHIE: Say what, Johnny?

JOHNNY: If it matters so much to you, Sophie, I just want to tell you that I can be pretty damn cruel myself. I can be disgusting. I could abuse you. Whatever you want.

SOPHIE: Oh. *(Pause)* What do you know. I was wrong about you. You're not one of those good people like I thought you were, Johnny. You're one of those who will do whatever they can to get what they want. An opportunist. I understand. Oh that's what you are.

(Turns to leave, sees BAL, *who has reentered. She turns back to* JOHNNY.*)*

SOPHIE: Johnny, I just remembered, Bal has asked me to ask you something.

*(*JOHNNY *nods, waits to be told.)*

SOPHIE: He wants you to start calling me Johanna. I have no idea why.

(She leaves. JOHNNY *turns to* BAL. *Silence)*

BAL: *(Shrugs; quietly)* You know me, Johnny—I can't help myself.

Scene Eight (b)

(A field. JOHNNY *and* SOPHIE *with the* BABY. BAL, *at a great distance, lies on his back, staring at the sky.)*

JOHNNY: *(To* BABY*)* Goo. Goo. Goo-goo. Cute.

SOPHIE: It's not crying. When it's not crying, I start to worry. I start waiting for it to cry. Then I try to shut it up. Then it shuts up and I worry.... It needs me.

JOHNNY: *(Playing with the* BABY*)* Tell me something, do you think I'm the type of person who would kill himself? Am I that type of person? *(Smiles at the* BABY*)* Am I?

SOPHIE: I wouldn't know.

JOHNNY: *(Without looking up)* But you do know. You know all about suicide.

SOPHIE: Do I? Mmmmmm. *(Picks up the* BABY*)* If I were to let it go, it would die. What a strange thought.

JOHNNY: *(Watching the* BABY*)* Well, I think I am the type. That's what I think. Gaga. Goo-goo. Pinky toes.... How do you think you'd react to my death, Johanna?

SOPHIE: Mmmmmm.

JOHNNY: *(To* BABY*)* Boo.

SOPHIE: I guess I'd be sad. Though my sadness would soon pass. Then I'd worry that my sadness passed too quickly, because I was brought up to feel sad for a long time. Or maybe I was brought up to feel bad that my sadness passes too quickly.

JOHNNY: Maybe. It's watching me.

SOPHIE: Yes.

JOHNNY: *(Playing with the* BABY*)* I love you, Johanna.

SOPHIE: I doubt it.

JOHNNY: *(Thinking seriously about it)* Maybe you're right, now that you mention it. Maybe I just want to take you away from him. Maybe all I'm really thinking is "beat him" and you're just the stakes. Maybe I'm thinking all I want is to see his face when you go away with me. I don't know. But that's what I'm thinking. And then I'm thinking—is that so bad? I'm thinking is that abnormal?

SOPHIE: You know who you sound like?

JOHNNY: Who? I'm always interested in how other people see me.

(The BABY *makes a noise.)*

SOPHIE: Goo. Goo. *(Cradling the* BABY*)* No doubt I'll slap it silly when it gets old enough to answer back.

JOHNNY: No doubt, Johanna. Goo. Goo.

Scene Eight (c)

(A plain. Cold. BAL, JOHNNY, *and* SOPHIE, *who carries the* BABY *in a sling across her front, enter.)*

BAL: It's getting dark, let's camp here.

JOHNNY: Bal, there's a village just up the way. Look, you can see the lights.

BAL: So?

JOHNNY: There'll be decent food in that village. And beds. Warm beds.

BAL: So?

JOHNNY: So then how can you make them sleep in the dirt another night when all we have to do is walk another ten, maybe fifteen minutes to make them and ourselves comfortable?

SOPHIE: Bal, we really wouldn't mind a bed now. And a bath. We'd kill for a hot bath.

BAL: Uh-huh.

JOHNNY: Then it's settled, let's go before it gets any darker.

BAL: No. I don't want to.

JOHNNY: For Christ's sake, why?

BAL: *(Quietly)* Two men and a woman with a baby. It'd look funny. People would talk. They'd stare. Innuendos would be made. I'd feel embarrassed. I might blush. I try to avoid situations like that.

JOHNNY: And that's your reason?

*(*BAL *nods.)*

JOHNNY:And what about her?

*(*BAL *shrugs.)*

JOHNNY: And the baby?

BAL: Okay, you've succeeded.

JOHNNY: Then we'll go into the village?

BAL: No. You succeeded in getting me to dislike myself.

*(*BAL *rubs his hands together, blows on them.* JOHNNY *turns away.)*

BAL: Cold.

(He stops rubbing, looks at SOPHIE, *walks up behind her, puts his arms around her and hugs. She presses her head against his shoulder.)*

BAL: Warm.

*(*JOHNNY *turns back, he is crying now.* BAL *looks at him, lets go of* SOPHIE, *and moves to* JOHNNY, *almost runs to him with arms outstretched and hugs him.* JOHNNY *cries on his shoulder.)*

BAL: Warm.

*(*SOPHIE *joins them and snuggles against them. The three hug.* BAL *moves away, feels his hands.)*

BAL: Better. *(He takes out a bottle, starts to drink, stops.)* Don't even bother to ask, there's only enough booze left for me.

*(*JOHNNY *and* SOPHIE *nod,* BAL *drinks.)*

JOHNNY: *(Touching his tears)* It's raining.

SOPHIE: *(Hugs the baby)* Warm.

BAL: *(Finishing the booze)* Better.

Scene Nine

(A tree. JOHNNY, *alone, sits on the ground with a long piece of rope. Throughout the beginning of the speech, he ties the rope into a noose.)*

JOHNNY: *(To the audience)* Honestly, I never dreamed I would find myself in a situation like this, and even if I had *imagined* the possibility, no doubt I would have imagined the experience of the situation to be quite different. I would have thought my head would be filled with images of my life. That is—I would have thought I'd be "seeing my life pass before me." Or another possibility—I would have thought I'd find some humor in my situation. I've read about certain individuals who have survived such experiences as this and who claim at the very last moment they found themselves funny. And they laughed. I can understand that. *(He finishes the knot, tries it on, takes it off, looks up at the tree.)* Or yet a third imaginable possibility would have been to be consumed by thoughts of my own funeral. Who would come? What would they say? Will I be missed? So—if someone would have come up to me a year or so ago and asked me what I would be thinking at the moment of my death, I no doubt would have said one of *these* possibilities—or perhaps some grouping of these possibilities. And I would have felt quite confident that I was correct. *(He throws the rope over the branch of the tree.)* However, I know now—from experience—how wrong I really would have been. Because my one urge now, in fact my only urge—is to talk. *(He puts the noose around his neck, climbs up on a stump.)* It's as if my mouth was the only chunk of me that is not yet ready to be nailed shut. It's like I'm just not talked out yet. So here—at the point of suicide—I find that my greatest concern is in finding something interesting to say. *(Pause. He tests the rope.)* So—what do I end up saying? What have I found to talk about? *Possibilities*—that's what. The possibility of imagining my life pass before me. The possibility of finding humor in my death. Possibilities. *(Pause)* You know, Johanna was wrong. She said I was one of those who will do whatever they can to get what they want. That's not me. I'm no opportunist. A man who thinks only about possibilities at the moment of his death is but one thing—an optimist. And that's just what I am. I am a hopeless optimist. That's me alright.

(He jumps. Blackout. Suddenly we hear a FEMALE SINGER *singing a sad song.)*

Scene Ten

(A nightclub. In the black we hear the final refrain of the sad song, then wild applause. BAL *and* CRONY *sit at a table.* CRONY *reads a newspaper.* FEMALE SINGER *stands next to* BAL. WAITER *stands at a distance.)*

FEMALE SINGER: I'm told you want to buy me a drink.

BAL: I do.

FEMALE SINGER: *(Sitting)* I haven't seen you around here before.

BAL: No.

*(*CRONY *turns a page.)*

FEMALE SINGER: Well, did you enjoy the show?

BAL: *(Perking up)* Your first song moved me. I was all yours. I followed every lyric.

FEMALE SINGER: *(Relaxes)* How wonderful.

BAL: *(Smiles)* Then with the second my mind began to wander. It did. I began to watch your throat. I began to watch how you breathed.

FEMALE SINGER: *(Uncomfortable)* Uh-huh.

BAL: Yes. And then I watched the lights. Then the people at other tables. By the third song I was lost in my own thoughts. I wondered whether I should leave. I wanted to be somewhere else.

FEMALE SINGER: What?!

BAL: *(Continuing)* I played with my ice.

FEMALE SINGER: You...?

BAL: ...played with my ice. By the fourth song I'd forgotten you. You were like traffic in the background.

FEMALE SINGER: *(Standing up, to* WAITER*)* Is this somebody's idea of a joke?!! *(She leaves.)*

BAL: *(Calling after her)* By the fifth song, you were a slight irritation. Like something in my eye. Like a pebble in my boot! *(He shrugs. Drinks)*

CRONY: *(Pointing to a picture in the paper)* Did you catch this? Poor boy—found hanging in the forest.

BAL: *(Looks. He is surprised.)* Johnny.

CRONY: You knew him?

BAL: I knew his girlfriend. *(Short pause)* So that's the kind of person he was.

CRONY: What kind of person is that?

BAL: The kind who can only take so much. *(Short pause)* I feel terrible. He shouldn't have killed himself. I wouldn't feel like this if he hadn't. *(Pause. He shakes his head, obviously upset. Then he suddenly notices his position.)* I remember seeing a movie once where a man sat in just such a position as this, holding just such a glass out in front of him. He talked to himself too. *(Pause)* Ever since then, this position has become for me—the drowning-one's-sorrows position. *(Breaks the position, nods)* We never stop learning how to behave. *(Works himself back into the "drowning-one's sorrows-position".)*

END OF PLAY

THE RETURN OF PINOCCHIO

for Seth Allen

THE RETURN OF PINOCCHIO was first presented in workshop at The Bay Area Playwrights Festival in the summer of 1982, directed by Richard Nelson and Robert Woodruff.

THE RETURN OF PINOCCHIO was produced by The Empty Space (M Burke Walker, Artistic Director) on 30 March 1983. The cast and creative contributors were:

PINOCCHIO .... Kurt Beattie
LUCIO .... Ruben Sierra
LUCIO'S WIFE .... Ruth McRee
LEONE .... Richard Riehle
MAMA .... Jayne Taini
SILIA .... Tina Marie Goff
ROSINA .... Suzy Hunt
CARLO .... Carlo Scaniuzzi
AMERICAN SOLDIER .... Reuben Renauldo Dumas

Director .... M Burke Walker
Set designer .... Scott Weldift
Costume designer .... Sheryl Collins
Lighting designer .... Michael Davidson
Sound designer .... Michael Holten

CHARACTERS & SETTING

PINOCCHIO, *a man in his thirties who once was a puppet who turned into a real boy.*
LUCIO
LUCIO'S WIFE
LEONE, *a newspaper editor*
MAMA, *his wife*
SILIA, *their daughter*
ROSINA
CARLO, *her son*
AMERICAN SOLDIER

The play takes place in 1946, first in a small village in Italy, later on a train in America.

Note: The title of each scene should be projected all the time the scene is played and should remain in view for a few moments after the scene is over.

Scene One
THE ARRIVAL

(Field near train tracks. Morning. A man leans against a stick. He smokes. Train whistle in the distance—getting closer. Man finishes the cigarette, with his fingers wets the end of the butt, then puts the butt into his mouth and chews. Train whistle closer. Suddenly a woman or girl's cry of pain is heard just offstage. Man flinches but controls himself and continues to stare off. Train noise very near now and suddenly a man in his thirties falls onto the stage—he has just jumped off the train. He wears a U S O uniform. He is PINOCCHIO.*)*

PINOCCHIO: *(To the train:)* Thank you, G I! *(To himself:)* I better make sure I didn't drop anything. *(Crawls around, then notices the man)* Hello.

(MAN *nods.)*

PINOCCHIO: Quite an entrance, huh? I jumped from that train. They wanted to stop for me—but orders are orders. But they slowed down.

MAN: Looked to me like they speeded up.

PINOCCHIO: Because they were coming down the hill. That's why they speeded up, but they speeded up less than they would have had they not slowed down so I could jump. That's what friends are for!

MAN: There are friends and then there are friends.

PINOCCHIO: Well, there aren't any better friends a man could have than my friends the G Is. What adventures we've had together. We've been through thick and thin. There's something real good about the Yanks, never seen boys who love a good time better than them. I'll give you a for-instance. I was on this train going between New York and Chicago. And there were these two G Is with me. Buddy, he was next to me, and Speed was sort of kitty corner—there's always somebody named Buddy or Speed in every crowd of Americans. No matter where you go you can call out those names and a Buddy or a Speed will answer and befriend you and take you home and his mother will make you soup and his sister who wears white socks will laugh at your jokes—her boyfriend's name is Bret and he's overseas, and the father, he slaps you on the back and gives you whiskey to see how well you can hold your liquor; anyway, there was this WAC who was sitting there too, on the train, she's facing me and all three of us guys, we'd been eyeing her, because American boys always eye girls on trains though they pretend to read books—mostly mysteries or books about accounting, because all American G Is plan to be accountants when the war is over—once they go through night school on the G I Bill—so you see we're looking at her and she has this run in her nylon; well—Buddy, and we know this, he has a pair of nylons in his suitcase—a brown suitcase with gold latches like all Americans have—and he was saving them for his girl, whose name is June and she's in California and she knits sweaters for the Red Cross—now that's a real American institution, the Red Cross, they have chapters all around the world; but we watch this WAC with the run and she notices us watching and we see she's uncomfortable, and we know why, because you see WAC's never have boyfriends so it's hard for them to get nylons, so she's uncomfortable, ashamed almost and you could even say sort of sad-looking. Well, Buddy looks at Speed, and Speed at me and me at Buddy, who now puts away his accounting book after using a playing card with a naked woman's picture on it as a bookmark, and after reaching up to get his suitcase and unlatching it, he takes out the nylons and puts his hand down in them. Well, Speed and I were chewing our fists to keep from laughing; and then he says to the WAC—her name is Heather, no I'm giving too much away, forget that I told you her name—and he says to her, I'm taking these home to my pa's farm, he likes to use 'em as feedbags for the horses. And at first she cringes, but then she laughs like American girls laugh when they're being teased, American girls just love to be teased, and we all laugh and then the Negro porter comes by to say the dining car is now open and then sort of shuffles away and later, in the dining car, and imagine our surprise when we learn that she's not a WAC at all but a WAVE and as WAVEs are almost always girls whose fathers have money—you see, that's why her name is Heather—she does have a boyfriend, but, as he's Jewish, she doesn't know if she'll marry him.

(Another cry of pain off.)

PINOCCHIO: What's that? There's a woman over there? What's she doing? Does she need help?

MAN: She's in control of the situation.

PINOCCHIO: She's with you then?

MAN: My wife.

PINOCCHIO: Oh. *(Short pause)* Well, I guess there's nothing like coming home to get you talking about your adventures.

MAN: Do I know you?

(For the first time the MAN *turns to look at* PINOCCHIO.*)*

PINOCCHIO: Lucio?! Lucio, is that you?!

(Tries to hug him, he pulls away)

PINOCCHIO: What's wrong? Aren't you happy to see me?

LUCIO: So you're back.

PINOCCHIO: Of course I'm back. I always come back, Lucio. Don't I always come back? Here, take an American cigarette.

(He takes one.)

PINOCCHIO: How is everyone? How's my Pa? Tell me everything that's happened.

LUCIO: There's nothing to tell.

PINOCCHIO: What are you talking about? You've lived through a war. You must have had some adventures.

*(*LUCIO'S WIFE *enters. She has a wire.)*

PINOCCHIO: Is this your wife, Lucio? Hey, not bad, Lucio. You know what they say in America?

LUCIO: *(To* WIFE:*)* Are you done?

WIFE: It's buried.

PINOCCHIO: What's buried?

WIFE: The kid.

PINOCCHIO: What kid?

WIFE: I gave myself an abortion.

PINOCCHIO: *(Reels back in shock)* Oh God! Why?

WIFE: We don't need more children. We have enough to do with the men.

(Pause)

PINOCCHIO: I see. I better get into town to see my father. We'll have a beer together, Lucio. *(Short pause)* I've brought American dollars with me. So we can have a beer together, Lucio.

*(*PINOCCHIO *leaves. Pause)*

LUCIO: You know who that is?

*(*WIFE *shakes her head.)*

LUCIO: His name's Pinocchio.

WIFE: Who's that?

LUCIO: His story's well known around here. His father was a cabinetmaker. One day he made a puppet and the puppet became alive. He was a naughty child and had many adventures, including once being swallowed by a great shark. Then a fairy turned him into a real boy, which was all he really wanted to be.

WIFE: What is this nonsense?!

LUCIO: No nonsense, it's true. He's very famous. Now he's come home from America. I thought I'd faint when I recognized him.

WIFE: Fairy tales!

LUCIO: Before the war such things were still possible. *(He starts to go.)*

WIFE: I gave myself an abortion and you give me miracles!
(She starts to throw the wire away.)

LUCIO: Keep the wire, we may need it to fix something.

(They leave.)

(End of Scene One)

Scene Two
THE ALPHABET

(A small room—the town newspaper office. LEONE, *the editor, sits at a table, setting type into a wooden galley.)*

LEONE: Damn. Where the hell is a "z"? *(Looks)* No, that's another "5". *(Puts it down)* Wait. *(Picks it up again and holds it to the light)* No "5". Mama, what did you do with my "z"s?!

MAMA: *(Off)* Check your pockets!

LEONE: My pockets? Why would I keep a "z" in my pocket? That woman has gone mad. I'm trying to typeset a newspaper, I can't find the letter I need, and my wife says to check my pockets. It's come to that. Life never prepared me for this. *(He checks his pockets.)* Nothing. Not even an "a", let alone a "z". Look what I'm doing. I'm taking orders from a crazy woman—is there no end to humiliation?

(Bell off. LEONE *doesn't notice it.)*

LEONE: I could just throw in a "q". Then it'd just look like a mistake—better that than having everyone think the town's newspaper is out of "z"s. I don't want to cause a panic.

*(*PINOCCHIO *has entered.)*

PINOCCHIO: Hello, Leone.

LEONE: *(Looks up, squints)* Who...? Oh my God! He's back!
(Jumps up, overturning the galley, letters fall to the floor)

PINOCCHIO: Here, let me help you.

LEONE: I don't believe my eyes! *(He walks over the letters.)*

PINOCCHIO: Be careful, you'll break them.

LEONE: Who cares? I should have stepped on them years ago.

PINOCCHIO: Leone, sit down.

LEONE: *(Stomping on the wooden letters)* What good are they? You can't eat them. I know because I tried.

PINOCCHIO: Let's just get them out of the way. *(Tries to push them under the table)*

LEONE: I broke this tooth on a "c".

PINOCCHIO: *(Half under the table)* Leone, it's good to see you.

LEONE: The writing was on the wall. First the "z"s, then the "r"s would be the next to go until finally it's the vowels. That's death for a newspaper; take away a man's vowels and what's left for him to say?

MAMA: *(Entering)* I found a "z"; it was in your other pants' pocket. *(Sees* PINOCCHIO*)* Ah! He's back? *(She drops the letter block and runs out.)*

LEONE: She found a "z"! *(He dives after it.)* She could have broken it. See what she thinks about newspapers? You can imagine what I've had to put up with in my marriage.

PINOCCHIO: Where did she go?

LEONE: To get you something to eat, of course. Everything hasn't changed.

PINOCCHIO: She doesn't have to do that. I can buy food. I have American dollars.

LEONE: That's right. You're a movie actor now.

PINOCCHIO: I wouldn't say that. There was only one movie and I played myself. You could hardly call that acting.

LEONE: But you're famous.

PINOCCHIO: Even in America, the story of a puppet who turns into a real boy is unique enough to cause some celebrity.

LEONE: And you got paid.

PINOCCHIO: I'd be embarrassed to say how much.

LEONE: So be embarrassed.

PINOCCHIO: Though I've tried also to pay back, in the best way I could, all that I was so fortunate enough to receive.

LEONE: You gave the dollars back?

PINOCCHIO: No. Americans don't give money back. What they do, you see, is use their money or their time to in some way help their fellow Americans, those who because of bad luck have not achieved the success which they themselves enjoy. See, America is like a giant kettle where all the races and nationalities of the world have come together to live in peace, and after a year or so when they are rich, they use their fortunes to build hospitals with their names on them, or great universities with ivy and their names on them, or they organize picnics for orphans—orphans being the least lucky Americans, that is until they grow up and can make their own luck. And me, being swept up in this American way, I joined the U S O and have been entertaining the G Is in Europe. It's what we in the movies do to give back a little something to America.

LEONE: So you kept the dollars.

PINOCCHIO: Of course. Leone, let me look at you. I can't tell you how many times I've thought of you, here in this shop, each week putting out your paper. How could I ever forget, when it was you, Leone, who first wrote about me and my adventures in your little paper.

LEONE: They were more than adventures, my boy. They were miracles! The kind that used to happen around here all the time. I'll tell you something—the fun went out of running a newspaper when the miracles stopped happening.

PINOCCHIO: But Leone, they're still happening. Every day of every week in a place called Hollywood, U S A. Oh, I know you've heard stories about pushy Americans groveling after every buck they can fit into their fat wallets...

LEONE: I've heard nothing. Tell me.

PINOCCHIO: And that gruff exterior is certainly a part of the American character, but before you criticize their ways....

LEONE: Who's criticizing?

PINOCCHIO: You must first look at what these tough Americans have accomplished, Leone. If you could only see with your own eyes Hollywood, you'd know to what purpose all this effort all this hard work has been exerted. Hollywood U S A—palm trees like in pictures, sunsets like in paintings, wide boulevards over which rumble cars the size of boxcars; the dramatic sweep of searchlights...

LEONE: We've had searchlights.

PINOCCHIO: The sky is blue, the grass green where once there was only brown desert; and the homes, Leone, and everyone owns at least one home, they are like palaces for kings, which is what Americans are, every man is his own king; and churches—Americans are very religious—each bigger than the next. Exotic fruits fall into your hands from trees which shade you from the sun....

(SILIA, LEONE's daughter has entered. She is pregnant.)

SILIA: Hello.

PINOCCHIO: Who's this? Don't tell me you're little Silia?

LEONE: When you go away, Pinocchio, people grow up.

PINOCCHIO: And get married as I can see.

SILIA: No.

PINOCCHIO: Oh. I see.

LEONE: It was either an American Negro sergeant. Or a lieutenant from Bavaria, or—who was the third possibility?

SILIA: A Sicilian laborer who had some stolen pork.

LEONE: You think it really could have been him? Those Sicilians are so greasy he probably slipped out.

PINOCCHIO: I think I better go.

LEONE: So soon? You just got here.

PINOCCHIO: I only came by to ask if you'd seen my father. I went to his shop but it was boarded up.

*(*SILIA *looks at* LEONE. *Pause.* MAMA *enters with food.)*

LEONE: Now you have to stay and eat or you'll hurt her feelings.

PINOCCHIO: Only a minute. But what were you going to say about my father?

(He sits. MAMA *places food in front of him, and stares at* PINOCCHIO.*)*

PINOCCHIO: Why is she staring?

LEONE: She's waiting for you to taste it. *(*PINOCCHIO *tastes the food.)*

MAMA: That'll be one American dollar for the food.

(He looks up.)

LEONE: And throw in two dollars more for damaging my type.

(End of Scene Two)

Scene Three
CARROTS

(A street. ROSINA, *a woman in her forties, pushes an almost empty vegetable cart. She stops the cart, pulls out a rag and wipes carrots. She has only two bunches. Afternoon)*

*(*PINOCCHIO *enters. Looks at her. Pause)*

PINOCCHIO: Hello.

ROSINA: Want to buy a carrot?

PINOCCHIO: It's me. Remember?

ROSINA: I don't need glasses. I have eyes.

PINOCCHIO: I'd thought you'd be surprised.

ROSINA: Word travels fast. You've been to Leone's.

PINOCCHIO: I guess I've forgotten what a small town this is.

ROSINA: Look behind you.

PINOCCHIO: *(Turns and looks toward the audience)* I know. Why do they keep following me? I've tried to find out, but the moment I start to get close they run away.

ROSINA: They're curious, to say nothing about hungry. Or maybe hungry, to say nothing about curious. You're famous.

PINOCCHIO: But this is my home. I grew up here. I couldn't be all that strange. They look at me like I'm from the stars.

ROSINA: Carrot?

*(*PINOCCHIO *takes one.)*

ROSINA: Ten American cents.

(He pays her; eats the carrot.)

ROSINA: When the Americans came in here, somehow it got out that here was the village of Pinocchio. I suspect it was Leone. The only smart thing he's ever done. How many letters did he lose today?

PINOCCHIO: He's always losing letters?

ROSINA: Hasn't published a paper in three years. He's always missing a letter. He never got into trouble.

PINOCCHIO: And my father, Rosina, what's happened to him?

ROSINA: *(After a pause)* We had no idea how famous you were. We hadn't heard about your American movie career. But when they all started clicking their cameras we started to understand. Every G I wanted a snapshot of the village of Pinocchio. Until then, we had no idea.

PINOCCHIO: Americans and their cameras! I know just what you mean. But what about my father, Rosina?

ROSINA: *(After a pause)* One of the G Is, a corporal, he wanted to fix up your father's shop and charge the other G Is to take pictures in there—of course it was my brother's barn that he fixed up in the end, because it was more in the middle of the village, but when he was done it almost looked like

Geppetto's shop, and he paid us to make puppets which he sold both here and shipped back to America. That was the best month of the war.

PINOCCHIO: There's nothing like American enterprise to make you see all that's possible. And that's a side of the American character that gets so much criticism. I for one just don't understand it.

*(*ROSINA *starts to push the cart away.)*

PINOCCHIO: Where are you going?

ROSINA: To earn a filthy penny.

PINOCCHIO: But what about my father, I'd hoped you would know where he is. You were, after all, his housekeeper.

ROSINA: *(After a pause)* I'd take you to him, but I have these carrots to sell.

PINOCCHIO: Here. *(Takes out money)* I'll buy them all. Now let's go.

ROSINA: You're going to eat all those carrots?

PINOCCHIO: No. I don't think so.

ROSINA: Then what are you going to do with them?

PINOCCHIO: Here. You can keep them. *(Gives her back the carrots)* Which way?

ROSINA: Later. I have these carrots to sell.

PINOCCHIO: *(After a pause)* Here. *(Takes out more money)* I'll buy them again. Now can we go?

ROSINA: *(Hands him the carrots)* What are you going to do with them?

PINOCCHIO: I'll eat them.

ROSINA: You can stuff your face with those hungry people watching you? *(She points toward the audience.)*

PINOCCHIO: Then I'll give them away.

ROSINA: You don't have enough for everybody. How are you going to decide who gets a carrot and who doesn't?

PINOCCHIO: *(After a pause, he suddenly throws the carrots into the audience.)* There!

(Sound of crowd fighting)

PINOCCHIO: *(Yells:)* Now take me to my father!

ROSINA: I'll have my son take you.

PINOCCHIO: Carlo?

ROSINA: You think I can afford more than one son?

PINOCCHIO: Why don't you take me?

ROSINA: *(Counting her money)* I want to go buy some cigarettes.

PINOCCHIO: *(Hands her some cigarettes)* Here. American.

ROSINA: Now I want to sell some cigarettes. American.

(Crowd continues to fight.)

(End of Scene Three)

Scene Four
AMERICAN CIGARETTES

(A cemetery. Wind. A single white cross. PINOCCHIO *and* CARLO *[early twenties] stand.* PINOCCHIO *stares at the cross.)*

(Pause)

CARLO: If you want to be alone.

PINOCCHIO: No. Stay. Please.

(Short pause, then he reaches into his pocket and pulls out a pack of cigarettes; he throws them toward CARLO *without looking at him.)*

(Pause)

*(*CARLO *looks at the cigarettes and then at* PINOCCHIO. *After a while he begrudgingly picks them up.)*

*(*PINOCCHIO *kneels before the grave and says a prayer in Latin. He crosses himself.)*

PINOCCHIO: *(Without looking at* CARLO*)* It's a nice spot. Who dug the grave?

CARLO: I did.

(Pause)

PINOCCHIO: Thank you. *(Short pause, then he reaches into his pocket and takes out another pack of cigarettes. He turns to* CARLO.*)* I appreciate it.

(Throws the pack to CARLO *who again hesitates and almost with hostility picks up the pack.)*

PINOCCHIO: Does anyone know how it happened?

CARLO: *(Shakes his head)* He was dumped out of a car. One minute he's in his shop and the next he's being dumped out of a car. He wasn't tortured. It was quick. One bullet.

PINOCCHIO: What did he do?

CARLO: He sold food. And he sold his food cheaper than others sold their food. So they informed on him.

PINOCCHIO: Someone from this village?

(CARLO *nods.)*

PINOCCHIO: One of his friends?

CARLO: We were all his friends.

PINOCCHIO: It's hard to understand. But I guess we have to try, don't we? Look at the Americans. They've never been invaded. Not one of them has seen their cities destroyed, seen the effects of war on their day-to-day life. *(Short pause)* And yet, damn it, they know that. They know how privileged or lucky they've been and they know how unfair it is to judge, to point that accusing finger at others who have been living in a hell that they themselves have never known. My father murdered by one of his own friends; but what right do I have to criticize—how do I know how I'd react in the same situation? It's hard, but you must just try to be fair, to understand, like the Americans do. What a fascinating people they are; aren't they always the first to help, to roll up their sleeves and plunge in with all the help they can give. Lost, they'll take you into their homes, a fire burning, soup on the table, feather quilt on the brass bed, a hot bath in a polished white ceramic tub; hungry, they will feed you, meat and potatoes and pumpkin pie; sick, they will nurse you, dabbing cool wet cloths across your hot forehead and when you wake up there's the mother of the house, a gentle smile on her face, her hair in a bun, her apron folded in her lap. Thank God I have been there and I have learned so much. *(He gets up.)* Carlo, I want to arrange for someone to distribute the boxes of clothes and canned foods I'll be sending back here. With a little food in their stomachs and clothes to be proud of instead of rags, who knows how much of this would have happened.

CARLO: Then you're going back?

PINOCCHIO: Tomorrow. I found who I was looking for. *(Short pause)* Carlo?

CARLO: Yes?

(Short pause)

PINOCCHIO: The miracles, is it true, they've all stopped happening?

CARLO: It is true.

PINOCCHIO: No more blood of St. Catherine in the village fountain? No wandering monks who change into ravens? No blind men to raise the dead? No talking birds? No flying fish?

CARLO: Nothing. Since the war.

PINOCCHIO: And that seems like a million years ago. No wonder everybody stares at me. I'm the last miracle they have. *(Starts to go. Stops. Turns back to the cross)* Damn it. He watched how I turned into a real boy, if only he could have seen how I've turned into a real man.

CARLO: Pinocchio?

PINOCCHIO: What is it? Oh right. *(He reaches for another pack of cigarettes)* Thank you. *(Gives them to him)*

CARLO: Pinocchio, there's something I should warn you about.

*(*PINOCCHIO *turns back.)*

CARLO: I heard my mother talking with some of her friends. The dollars you have, they were talking about how they were going to steal them from you.

PINOCCHIO: My dollars? How?

CARLO: During the night, they'll come to when you're sleeping. And the fattest, I heard, will sit on you; and the strongest, I heard this too, will cover your mouth so you can't scream, and my mother, who is the quickest, will take the dollars.

PINOCCHIO: Like the blind cat and the crippled fox.

CARLO: Who?

PINOCCHIO: They're an adventure from my youth—when thieves were cats and foxes instead of old women making a living on the black market. Where can I hide until morning?

CARLO: No where. Everybody's watching you.

PINOCCHIO: Then my dollars. I'll hide my dollars. You must know a good hiding place.

CARLO: I have a secret place where I keep some of my things.

PINOCCHIO: Take me there.

CARLO: It's secret.

PINOCCHIO: Then here, you hide the dollars for tonight, and bring them to me in the morning.

(Starts to give him the money)

CARLO: Are you sure you trust me?

PINOCCHIO: I trust you.

(Turns away, quickly turns back, hands him another pack of cigarettes)

PINOCCHIO: I trust you. *(He goes.)*

(End of Scene Four)

Scene Five
SIZZLING STEAKS

(Cafe. Table. Two chairs. Coat rack. Almost dawn)

(PINOCCHIO *with a bottle and glass in front of him. He is drunk.)*

PINOCCHIO: Set 'em up! One more! One more for the road! *(Points in a direction. Short pause, then points in another direction, as if he were figuring out which was the right road)* For the road! *(He reaches for the bottle, knocks it over, but catches it just in time, smiles about how quick he was. Then without looking he pours the bottle onto the table, missing his glass. Drinks from the glass. Wipes his mouth.)* Ah! Getting sort of warm in here. *(Loosens his tie. Struggles to take off his jacket, finally does and goes to the coat rack to hang it up. He misses. Bumps into the rack)* Excuse me. My fault. *(Hangs coat up, but the rack falls on him)* Fresh! *(Sets the rack back up, starts to move, stops, takes off his hat, looks around where to put it, notices one of the arms of the rack, sets his hat on it)* Thank you. *(Reaches into his pocket for a tip, tries to hand the rack a coin, lets it drop)* There's more where that came from, cutie. *(Walks back to the table; referring to the rack:)* Nice tits.

(Almost falls, recovers; SILIA *has watched the end of this; she has entered with another bottle. He now notices the bottle is empty.)*

PINOCCHIO: One more! And another one for the skinny girl there. *(Points to the coat rack. Pause.)* I said one more. Jesus H Christ, who's a fella got to fuck to get a drink around here?

SILIA: Are you sure you haven't had enough?

PINOCCHIO: Who are you talking to? Someone around here giving you trouble? Who's the loud mouth who's giving this lady trouble? Just have me talk to him.

SILIA: It's nearly dawn. You don't want to sleep?

PINOCCHIO: Sleep? So you can do what? Gotch you! Gotch you! Ha-ha. You fucking wops. You fucking dago wops. You fucking dago wops wait 'til he goes to sleep and roll him thieves. See. Gotch you. Ha-ha. What do you think, that I'm made of money? You want a handout, then stick out your hand! Here. *(Reaches into his pocket, throws some coins on the ground)* Leave that for the cleaning lady. Or bring along all your barefoot little dagos—that is, if they can take a break from sticking their hands into other people's back pockets, or from selling themselves to fat old men to play with. Wait—no—that's the Greeks, not you dagos. Excuse me. Even a man who works for a living makes a mistake now and then. And I've made every red cent I have. Nobody's given me nothing. I don't walk around with my head down living in buildings that's all rubble. I take pride in my surroundings. You got weeds growing everywhere. You see what I'm saying? Am I getting through inside your head? You little weasels I never know what you're thinking. You walk so slow it's like you don't want to get anywhere; you spend half your life slapping mackerels, well what the hell do you wops pray for anyway—for some fat American to bail you out? Well, we'll do it once, but by golly you're on your own after that. Well, we'll just pick up our technology and leave you to pinch each other's ass in the beautiful Mediterranean sun! We don't need you—you need us! And the sooner you understand that, the better it'll be for you! I'm tired of taking your shit, what I want is a goddamn thank you. *(He goes to get his coat)*

SILIA: You leaving, Pinocchio?

PINOCCHIO: I'm going back to where a man can sleep under the stars, have a saddle for a pillow and keep his gun at his side. And if any rustler or fox or Italian woman wants to sneak up on him, let them try, 'cause they're gonna get a bullet through the face. And I'm not talking cities now, they're just the same shitholes as this dago swamp—I don't want any Negro making eyes at my wife; or if he does I hope to God I'm there. *(Short pause)* No, I'm going where things are open and there's nobody trying to climb on my back, where the only weight you got to carry is your own. And your families. I'm going where for dinner you cut off a nice two-inch steak and you sizzle it on an open fire with the smoke and smell swirling in the moon light. You ever have a two-inch sizzling steak? *(No response)* I'm talking to you. Have you? I'm asking, have you?! How the hell can you call yourself a human being when you haven't had a two-inch sizzling steak?!! I don't know what's wrong with you people. *(He sits.)* You make me ashamed. I'm so ashamed. *(He passes out.)*

(Pause)

*(*SILIA *looks at him, then at the coat rack. She goes to the jacket and checks all the pockets—she finds a few coins and takes them. She turns to go, stops, goes back to the jacket and takes it and puts it over* PINOCCHIO*'s shoulders like a blanket. She pats it. And leaves)*

(End of Scene Five)

Scene Six
FOOD

*(*ROSINA *beside her cart. Morning. She smokes.)*

*(*CARLO *enters.)*

ROSINA: Where have you been?

CARLO: On the hill watching the new Americans arrive. Did you know they were coming?

ROSINA: Lucietta told me.

CARLO: Aren't you interested?

ROSINA: I was when Lucietta told me. Do I have to be interested when you tell me too? Besides, we've nothing left to sell. And what good are Americans when you've nothing left to sell?

CARLO: I saw them unload the trucks. There must have been a mile of them. One... *(He stops, looks off.)* Sh-sh. *(He ducks behind the cart.)*

(PINOCCHIO enters.)

PINOCCHIO: Have you seen your son? He was supposed to meet me this morning.

ROSINA: You think I can keep track of him?

PINOCCHIO: If he comes by, tell him I'm looking for him. *(He hurries off.)*

CARLO: *(Standing up)* One—or at least one—was packed in ice. When they opened the door, all these chunks of ice fell out. That must be where they keep the meat.

ROSINA: And the butter.

CARLO: And the butter.

ROSINA: Also the cheese.

CARLO: Do Americans eat cheese?

ROSINA: In little bits when they have their cocktails.

CARLO: Swiss?

ROSINA: No, American.

CARLO: Oh... And then they were unloading another truck and I saw them drop a crate. It smashed wide open. It was packed with cans.

ROSINA: Dented now.

CARLO: The cans?

ROSINA: I've been told Americans won't eat from dented cans.

CARLO: If they're hungry enough they would.

ROSINA: If they were hungry enough they would.

(MAMA runs in, with a basket.)

MAMA: The Americans are back, did you hear?

ROSINA: We heard.

CARLO: I saw them.

MAMA: Do you know how long they'll stay?

CARLO: They're putting up fences.

MAMA: Then they'll be here a month at least.

ROSINA: What's in the basket?

MAMA: I emptied out the barn. You never know what these Americans will buy.

ROSINA: You cleaned out your barn so many times, what could be left to sell?

MAMA: You never know.

CARLO: They've got trucks stuffed with meat. I saw the ice.

MAMA: Any fish?

ROSINA: You're getting picky?

MAMA: No. No. Meat's fine too.

CARLO: And American cheese, we think.

MAMA: What's that?

CARLO: It's not Swiss.

ROSINA: It's big. It comes only big, like everything American.

*(*CARLO *ducks again;* PINOCCHIO *enters.)*

PINOCCHIO: You still haven't seen him?

MAMA: Who?

PINOCCHIO: Carlo.

MAMA: What do you want him for?

PINOCCHIO: He was doing me an errand. We were supposed to meet up this morning before I leave.

MAMA: You're leaving?

PINOCCHIO: I have no reason to stay.

MAMA: Did you hear that the Americans have come back?

PINOCCHIO: Where?

MAMA: Over the hill. Thousands of them. And trucks too.

ROSINA: Crammed with meat.

MAMA: And maybe fish.

ROSINA: And maybe butter.

MAMA: I'm going to sell my last belongings to the Americans.

ROSINA: You won't get a penny for that junk.

MAMA: We'll see who's eating fish tonight.

PINOCCHIO: I'll go take a look on the hill. Maybe he's watching the Americans.

MAMA: Good idea. I'll bet that's just where he is.

PINOCCHIO: But if you see him...

ROSINA: We'll be sure to tell you.

(PINOCCHIO *goes off.)*

(CARLO *stands again.)*

MAMA: *(To* CARLO*)* What was that about?

CARLO: Who knows? He probably wants to say goodbye, give me a nice firm handshake, pat me on the back, and tell me to work hard and be good.

MAMA: Then I don't blame you for avoiding him.

ROSINA: Where's Leone?

MAMA: He's trying to start his truck.

ROSINA: He's going to sell it again?

MAMA: He'll keep selling it as long as he can keep stealing it back.

ROSINA: I wish I had a husband with a truck.

MAMA: The war's been especially cruel to you, Rosina.

ROSINA: Look—there's Lucietta.

MAMA: Oh, God. Where did she get that dress?

ROSINA: *(Calls)* Hello!

MAMA: Hello! Yes, we heard! Good luck!

ROSINA: She doesn't give up.

MAMA: Let her dream.

ROSINA: No American in his right mind would marry her. She hasn't a prayer.

MAMA: She'd take a crazy one.

ROSINA: Now your Silia is another story.

MAMA: She's been close twice.

ROSINA: I didn't know that.

MAMA: But in the end they only wanted a virgin.

ROSINA: Why a virgin?

MAMA: American men only marry virgins.

ROSINA: I didn't know that.

MAMA: That's because you don't have a daughter.

CARLO: When you two are finished let me know, because I want to tell you what else I heard.

ROSINA: What did you hear?

CARLO: I talked to one of the sentries and....

*(*LEONE *enters.)*

LEONE: I got the truck started. It should run a good thirty, maybe forty minutes before it falls apart again. Going to have to talk fast to sell it this time.

MAMA: Leone, Carlo's seen meat. And maybe fish.

CARLO: They have trucks packed with ice.

LEONE: You saw meat?

CARLO: I saw the ice.

LEONE: You think they have any mushrooms?

ROSINA: How can you think about mushrooms at a time like this when there's meat?

LEONE: When I think of meat I think also about mushrooms. Can't a man dream?

CARLO: They have cans—so maybe they have canned mushrooms.

LEONE: It'd be better if they were fresh. But I won't turn my nose up.

*(*CARLO *ducks again.)*

*(*PINOCCHIO *enters.)*

PINOCCHIO: Amazing, isn't it? Almost beautiful. They're like a giant graceful machine—they way they've set up camp so quickly. Just yesterday I was standing on that hill looking at a brown field. And this morning—there are tents, even a building, fences. Tell me what other nation's army could work such miracles? *(Short pause)* They're resting now. But even when they rest they can't help being active. There were a group of soldiers playing catch—their shirts off and their dog tags catching the sun. And over in another corner, I could see the Negro soldiers. I wasn't close enough to hear, but by the way they were moving, I'll bet anything they were singing. What energy those people have. It's just astonishing. *(Starts to go; stops)* He wasn't there. I'm starting to get worried. He was doing me a favor. I hope to God nothing has happened to him. I'd feel just terrible. *(He goes.)*

*(*CARLO *stands up.)*

LEONE: Who's he talking about?

MAMA: Him.

LEONE: He's looking for you?

CARLO: Forget about him. Let me finish what I was telling you.
I talked to a sentry.

MAMA: And?

CARLO: And we've been declared off limits to the camp.

LEONE: Who's we?

CARLO: Us. The whole village.

MAMA: You're joking.

CARLO: I wish I was.

ROSINA: How are we supposed to eat?

LEONE: Why?

CARLO: They're worried about our black markets. That there is more than just a camp, it's supply headquarters for the whole regiment.

LEONE: That's why the meat.

MAMA: And the fish.

CARLO: And ice.

LEONE: What a pity. And I was just beginning to smell that meat.

CARLO: Maybe we can still do more than just smell it. I have an idea.
We'll need your truck.

LEONE: Take it. What good is it if I can't sell it? There's no place I want to go in it.

MAMA: What's your idea?

CARLO: The sentry I know can be bribed.

ROSINA: Bribed? With what?

(PINOCCHIO enters.)

PINOCCHIO: I'm getting really worried now. Maybe we could organize a search. If anything's happened to that boy, it's on my conscience.... *(Sees CARLO)* Carlo? There you are. God, I'm happy to see you.
Why didn't you tell me he was here? Did you know I was looking for you?

CARLO: No.

PINOCCHIO: I wanted to say goodbye.

CARLO: Goodbye.

(CARLO stares at PINOCCHIO.)

PINOCCHIO: *(Uncomfortable)* Then I'll go. *(Starts to move)* Oh, I nearly forgot—do you have my...uh....

CARLO: Your what?

PINOCCHIO: What I gave you to keep for me.

CARLO: I don't know what you're talking about. *(To the others)* Let's go.

PINOCCHIO: Carlo, my money. *(Pause)*

CARLO: What money?

(They stare at each other.)

(Long pause)

*(*CARLO *finally turns and goes.)*

PINOCCHIO: Carlo, but that isn't fair.

(End of Scene Six)

Scene Seven
AMERICAN MILLIONAIRES

(Cafe. Chairs set on the table. Late afternoon)

*(*PINOCCHIO*, with a mop, washes the floor.* SILIA*, with broom, sweeps. Pause as they work)*

SILIA: It's good of you to work off your bar bill like this.

PINOCCHIO: What choice do I have?

SILIA: You could have just left. Who would have stopped you?

PINOCCHIO: I always pay what I owe. You have to. If people stopped paying their debts, the world would collapse. I don't want that on my shoulders. *(Mops)*

SILIA: The world? The whole world?

PINOCCHIO: That part which is civilized, that is. If men stopped paying what they owed, the entire free enterprise system would go down the drain. And it wouldn't take much either—it's a beautiful yet fragile organism. It wouldn't take much to kill it. Just say I didn't pay back Signora Sara. Would she give credit to the next customer? I doubt it. No, it'd be cash in advance. So without credit, the demands upon hard currency would be so great that the value of a dollar would be in fact greater than its purchasing power—so prices would fall and you'd have a depression. Of course, more money would then be printed to try to compensate and than you'd have inflation. No, Silia, once you stop paying your debts you are asking for chaos, and, as chaos is the incubator of communism, you are in fact asking for communism. So you see, it's not out of any moral sense of responsibility that I'm mopping this floor—I'm not getting on any high horse doing this—I'm only doing what I consider to be my duty—to keep the free enterprise system from crumbling and to keep the world from the Reds.

SILIA: God!

PINOCCHIO: In America they think about things like that. All the time. *(Mops)* It's also my hope that my mopping here might serve as some sort of example. I'd be lying if I said that wasn't my hope as well. This village, I'm afraid, is nudging toward that abyss of chaos; maybe a little of what I'm saying, and what my actions are showing, will rub off here. I can at least hope. What time is it?

*(*SILIA *checks a clock.)*

SILIA: Nearly five.

PINOCCHIO: Another hour and my debt will be cleared. You know, Silia, this village—and that means all of you—are going to have to face some tough decisions. America's not going to bail you out forever. Sooner or later it's going to have to come from you people. I know it won't be easy, but the other scenario isn't a pretty picture either. You people are on a free ride now, but don't think it's always going to be this way. Americans are as generous as any people in the world, but they don't like to feel like suckers. Show them that you're trying and they'll be there to lend a shoulder, but try to take them for a ride and good luck. They can be ruthless.

SILIA: You really care, don't you?

PINOCCHIO: You have to. Everyone has to. When people stop caring, you might as well throw in the cards. No one ever said it was going to be easy. It takes a lot of grit and sweat and good old-fashioned determination. That's how you turn things around. You know, I've half a mind to stay here just to show you people how it's done.

SILIA: How what's done?

PINOCCHIO: How to pull yourself up by your own bootstraps. How to dream. How to make something out of yourselves.

SILIA: But there's nothing here. There's hardly even any food.

PINOCCHIO: So you start with nothing. It doesn't mean you won't end up with a lot. Look at me here—I'm making what—twenty-one cents an hour. It's a start. And if I played my cards right, I could turn those twenty-one cents into a million dollars inside of two years.

SILIA: From mopping floors?

PINOCCHIO: Every American millionaire started without much more. Mopping floors, washing dishes, selling newspapers. Once you got your toe in the door, all that can keep you from kicking it in is yourself. That's what people here don't understand. It's all "Give me, give me": I've never seen so many hands out in my life. All of you're looking for the quick buck, instead of looking into yourselves to find that fortune that's out there all right, just waiting for you to pick it up.

SILIA: But twenty-one cents an hour?

PINOCCHIO: That's where you start. The rules are so simple every American child knows them by heart like the pledge of allegiance. You start with twenty-one cents, you put in twelve, fifteen, twenty hours a day—sure, it's not easy, but who said it would be—you offer to sleep on the floor, that way you don't pay rent and you eat scraps and warmed-over scraps, and three-day-old scraps, saving every penny, penny by penny, that you can save. So you got about five dollars now and you start to look for an investment. Something with a high yield, nothing blue chip, it's a gamble, but that's the name of the game—you keep your eye open for some business that's in trouble, maybe a newsstand and you buy in with five dollars and a lot of your time, course you keep mopping floors, so now you're working maybe twenty-two hours a day, but you take the night shift so you can sleep without anybody knowing that you're sleeping; so you're putting more and more dollars into the newsstand, and by sheer stamina you are wearing your partner down—preferably he's an old man without much ambition left in him, and without any sons—so you become like a son to him so he trusts you, and so he doesn't question when you split your interest in the newsstand and sell half for twenty bucks which you immediately invest in a share of a shoe store; course, you collect the twenty fast and drag your feet on paying the twenty to the shoe store owner, because during that delay you can loan the twenty out at short term to some widow or family with a sick mother who needs the cash fast and are willing to pay good interest—and you make them pay up when the shoe store owner threatens to go to court; so now you own a part of a shoe store, a part of a newsstand and you got a reputation in the neighborhood for short-term loans. Now of course you're still mopping floors so the next five dollars you save you open another newsstand across the street from the one you partially own and try to drive the old man and your other partner out of business. You take a bath for a month by undercutting their prices—you're selling the Tribune now for one cent and giving away free coffee. The old man who's like a father to you can't hold his own now, his customers are now your customers and they may be looking sheepish when they buy from you but who can pass up that free cup of coffee? So you make an offer to buy full control of the old man's newstand—for five bucks—on credit—he sells and so you burn it down to collect the insurance—fifty bucks you get because you went to the biggest insurance company you could find and it wasn't worth their bother to investigate. So you got forty-five dollars now in cash—you paid the old man the five—see, that's what I was telling you about always paying what you owed—and a newsstand that sells coffee for a dime and the Trib for four cents and part of a shoe store and you're still mopping floors.

So you follow a similar scenario with the shoe store but instead of burning it down you open a new shop as a discount store, which means you just raise the prices in the other store and you call yourself a chain. You start giving credit called "lay-a-way plan", which means they pay some now and the rest later, but if they don't pay the rest later, you keep the money they've already put down. If they don't like it, let them sue. This inability to pay is highly likely if you've picked the right neighborhood. So what you have is a pure profit, which of course you invest in short-term loans. Now, should they come up with the rest of the payment, you stall them on delivering their goods because you haven't yet purchased their goods yourself or if you have you've sold them already.

So you're still mopping floors—but not for much longer—and you've got a newsstand empire and a chain of shoe stores and a loan business on the side where you charge nine-point-nine percent—ten percent is against the law in American, ten percent is considered usury. But the road is not as smooth as you might think. Health inspectors are starting to look into the stands where you are also selling hot dogs now, and fire marshals are on your back because all your back exits in your shoe shops have been covered by inventory—space after all is at a premium. So here's one of the big hurdles you are going to have to face—in America there are so many god damn regulations, I don't know how the government expects a man to make an honest buck. I wish it would just get off our backs, but it won't so you finally realize you need political connections. But you are still a small fry—so what can you do for them? Except maybe give them a free meal every now and then. So one day you throw down your mop and walk into the office of the restaurant owner and toss an envelope full of greenbacks on his desk and buy him out.

That's the last mopping you do—if you've gotten married to a nice girl who believes in you and stands beside you, you give her the mop, as you know what twenty-onc cents an hour can mount to and you don't want some smart-ass kid in there breathing down your neck. So you've stopped mopping, and you've diversified your investments, so your collateral is top drawer, but you still have only fifty bucks in hard cash in your pocket; so one day you walk into Chase Manhattan Bank and take out a loan for twenty thousand dollars and start to play with the big boys in the open market—while keeping up the insurance just to hedge your bet, and you open an office on Madison Avenue, hire an English secretary and change your name to Robert Buckingham. And there you have it—an American millionaire in the making! *(Pause)*

SILIA: But you only have twenty thousand, how do you make the rest?

PINOCCHIO: With an office on Madison Avenue, with an English secretary and a name like Robert Buckingham, you can't fail to become a millionaire in America.

(Long pause. They work.)

SILIA: And the wife? She's still mopping the floor at the restaurant?

PINOCCHIO: He probably divorced her.

SILIA: Oh, God, why? I liked her.

PINOCCHIO: She got fat. American millionaires like skinny women. With high cheek-bones.

(Pause)

SILIA: Oh.

(They work.)

SILIA: But how could he divorce her, isn't he Catholic?

PINOCCHIO: He bought a new stained glass window for a seminary in Westchester County.

(Noise of the truck off. SILIA *looks out the window.)*

SILIA: It's Carlo and Father. Where can they be going?

(End of Scene Seven)

Scene Eight
THE CRIME

*(*LEONE*'s newspaper office. Table. Three chairs.* LEONE *and* CARLO *at the table. Beef on the table.)*

(Evening)

(Pause)

CARLO: Should I serve?

LEONE: Wait for Mama. *(Short pause.* CARLO *sniffs.)*

CARLO: Smell.

*(*LEONE *sniffs.* CARLO *runs his finger across the beef and licks his finger.)*

CARLO: Here, let me give you a taste. While we're waiting for Mama.

LEONE: While we're waiting.

*(*CARLO *cuts a small piece, gives it to* LEONE, *who eats;* LEONE *groans with pleasure.)*

LEONE: Here. Let me give you a slice.

(Cuts a slice, gives it to CARLO, *who eats and groans.)*

LEONE: American.

CARLO: How can you tell?

LEONE: Process of elimination. Who else has beef? Mushroom?

*(*CARLO *takes a mushroom.* LEONE *takes a few.)*

CARLO: How many are you taking?

LEONE: I took two. Here, take another so we'll be even.

CARLO: You took three.

LEONE: One was just the stem. Easy on the sauce.

CARLO: Maybe I should carve. Unless, of course, you...?

LEONE: No. No. Carve. *(Short pause)* By all means carve.

*(*CARLO *carves.)*

CARLO: Your plate.

*(*LEONE *hands him his plate;* CARLO *serves.)*

(Pause)

(Suddenly they look at each other and start laughing—they laugh to the point of hysterics—then start eating, shoveling the food in, groaning. They eat like they've been starving.)

MAMA: *(Entering with a plate)* The potatoes are done. You didn't wait for me!

LEONE: *(With his mouth full)* It was getting cold.

MAMA: It wasn't getting cold. I said, it wasn't getting cold.

LEONE: I don't have time to talk to you now.

*(*MAMA *digs in and eats like the other two.)*

CARLO: Where's the butter?

LEONE: Didn't you get the butter?

CARLO: I wasn't supposed to get the butter.

LEONE: I got the mushrooms.

(They eat.)

MAMA: *(With her mouth full)* Where's your mother?

CARLO: She said she wanted to eat alone so she could enjoy it more.

LEONE: I can understand that.

MAMA: *(To* CARLO*)* Slow down. That's your third piece.

(They eat.)

(Bell off. After a pause, PINOCCHIO *enters. No one notices; he watches them.)*

PINOCCHIO: *(Finally:)* Where did all that come from?

(They look up but keep eating.)

PINOCCHIO: I thought the American camp was off limits.

(They ignore him.)

PINOCCHIO: Carlo, do you have anything for me?

CARLO: Only enough for the three of us.

PINOCCHIO: That's not what I'm talking about. And you know it.

(Pause. They eat.)

PINOCCHIO: How could you do it, Carlo? You think you can just steal and get away with it? *(Pause)* You think the world owes you something, Carlo? You've got a big shock ahead of you, if you think that.

LEONE: What do you what? Can't you see we're eating?

PINOCCHIO: I came to say goodbye.

MAMA: *(With mouth full)* He's leaving.

PINOCCHIO: Tonight.

(Pause)

LEONE: I'd shake your hand, but mine's greasy.

(They eat.)

*(*PINOCCHIO *leaves.)*

CARLO: How could you have forgotten the butter? It's a crime.

(End of Scene Eight)

Scene Nine
THE BLOOD OF SAINT CATHERINE

*(*ROSINA*'s cart. Morning. Bright sun.* ROSINA *sits and leans against her cart, her eyes closed.* LEONE *enters, he walks slowly. After a while he looks at* ROSINA*.)*

LEONE: Sleep well?

ROSINA: I slept content. *(Wipes the air in front of her face.)* Gnats. They smell my breath. *(Giggles)*

LEONE: You know how I slept?

ROSINA: Just tell me.

LEONE: Like an American. Ever seen an American sleep?

ROSINA: Don't get personal.

LEONE: They sleep with little smiles across their faces. And they don't have nightmares.

ROSINA: No?

LEONE: Only dreams.

ROSINA: So what did you dream about?

LEONE: I was on the side of a hill. And I was plowing. Suddenly my mule—I had a mule—it broke away from me. I tried to chase it, but the lightning made it run fast. It started to rain cats and dogs. The field was all mud, and I was up to my knees in it. I tried to pull at my boots but slipped, and that's when I found out....

ROSINA: Found out what?

LEONE: That the mud was chocolate. Swiss chocolate.

ROSINA: So you kept eating right through your sleep.

LEONE: The whole time. I can still taste that chocolate.

ROSINA: And the rain, was it wine?

LEONE: No. No. Just rain.

ROSINA: Too bad. And Mama?

LEONE: She wasn't in my dream.

ROSINA: Did she sleep well?

LEONE: She slept at the table. With her head on a plate. If I'd had an apple, I would have put it in her mouth. *(Laughs)* Where's Carlo, we were going to go back to the camp this morning.

ROSINA: He's probably still in bed, dreaming of chocolate like you.

LEONE: Is that how you left him?

ROSINA: *(Shrugs)* I slept out here last night. And I watched the stars.

LEONE: And the moon that looks like cheese.

(A woman's scream in the distance. They look at each other.)

WIFE: *(From the first scene. Off)* Hurry! Hurry! Come!

ROSINA: *(To* LEONE*)* What is it?

LEONE: I don't know.

WIFE: *(Running in)* Hurry. Come quick. Go look! Look!

LEONE: Look at what?

(He grabs her, she is crying.)

WIFE: Get a priest! *(She falls on her knees.)*

(Church bells begin to toll.)

LEONE: What's going on?

(He runs off. WIFE *on her knees prays in Latin.)*

ROSINA: You, watch my cart.

(She starts to run off, MAMA *hurries in.)*

MAMA: *(To* WIFE*:)* What is it, an air raid?

ROSINA: Ask her. I don't know. *(She runs out.)*

MAMA: What did you see? Quit that and tell me, what did you see?

WIFE: Get a priest. Hurry! It's happened! *(Continues to pray, bell continues to toll.)*

MAMA: *(More to herself)* What's happened? *(Looks up at the sky)* I don't hear any planes.

WIFE: Get a priest and pray. It's a miracle.

MAMA: What's a miracle? Where's everyone running to? What did you see?!

WIFE: A miracle!

LEONE: *(Running in)* It's a miracle!

MAMA: What is? Where? *(Stopping him)*

LEONE: The fountain. Where's Silia? She should see this. She wasn't old enough before, but now she is.

MAMA: Leone, what are you talking about? What is happening?!

LEONE: Go look at the fountain. Go!

MAMA: What is it?

LEONE: The water's turned to blood!

MAMA: Oh, my God. Saint Catherine's blood?

LEONE: Of course!

MAMA: It's a miracle? Where's Silia, she should see this. *(She runs out.)*

WIFE: Get a priest!

LEONE: *(To* WIFE:*)* Who knows about this? Do the Americans know? They'll kill just to pay to see this. We should put up a fence. So we can control the crowds. Where's Carlo? Carlo!!!

ROSINA: *(Hurries in)* And you said there'd be no more miracles.

LEONE: When did I say that?

ROSINA: You and everybody else. How dare you call yourselves Catholics. Look. *(Shows her hand, which has blood on it)*

LEONE: You touched it?

ROSINA: Of course I touched it. I have arthritis, don't I? *(She goes to her cart.)*

LEONE: Don't you think we should put up a fence?

ROSINA: What do we need a fence for?

LEONE: To make sure everyone pays.

ROSINA: I'll have Carlo help you.

LEONE: What are you doing?

ROSINA: *(Taking bottles from the cart)* If it can cure arthritis, who knows what drinking it can do. *(She starts to run off.)*

LEONE: Wait. Do you have any more bottles?

ROSINA: Find your own. *(She runs off.)*

LEONE: My wife has some bottles. *(Starts to go)*

MAMA: *(Entering)* Leone, where are you going?

LEONE: Go get some bottles.

MAMA: What for?

LEONE: Do you know how much that blood is worth?

*(*MAMA *starts to run off.)*

WIFE: Did they get a priest?

MAMA: *(Over her shoulder while she's running)* One's coming. *(She leaves.)*

LEONE: Wait. Were you the first to see it?

WIFE: I don't know.

LEONE: Did you see it turn from water to blood?

WIFE: I don't know. It was blood when I walked by.

LEONE: Did you hear any voices?

WIFE: Voices?

LEONE: Sometimes with a miracle you also hear voices.

WIFE: I don't know. Maybe.

LEONE: You know, they could make you a saint for this.

WIFE: A saint? Oh, God. Where's the priest? *(She hurries off toward the fountain.)*

MAMA: This is all I could carry, there's more in the shed.

LEONE: Did you find Silia?

MAMA: She wasn't home.

LEONE: Then she's going to miss it.

MAMA: Maybe it'll last.

LEONE: The first miracle since before the war, don't hold your breath.

MAMA: *(Looking off)* What's she doing?

LEONE: She jumped in. She wants to be a saint.

MAMA: She could defile the blood. Stop her!

ROSINA: *(Enters with filled bottles)* That woman's going to ruin it for all of us. Who's going to want to drink blood that she's been swimming in.

LEONE: How much did you get?

ROSINA: A couple of liters. But I'm running low on bottles. How much do you want for your tub?

MAMA: It's not for sale.

*(*WIFE *suddenly lets out a piercing scream, off.)*

(Pause)

(The bells continue.)

ROSINA: What happened?

LEONE: Oh, Christ. *(He runs to the fountain.)*

ROSINA: What is it, I can't see?

MAMA: It's a body.

ROSINA: A body? Another miracle? A body rising from the blood of St Catherine. Dear God. *(Crosses herself)* Let's go see.

(They move.)

MAMA: Wait.

ROSINA: *(Pulling at* MAMA*)* Let's get closer.

*(*LEONE *hurries in.)*

LEONE: *(To* MAMA*)* Hold her back.

*(*MAMA *grabs* ROSINA.*)*

ROSINA: Let me go. Why can't I see? What is it? *(Fighting now)* What is it?

LEONE: It's Carlo.

ROSINA: Carlo?

ROSINA: It's his blood. His throat was cut from ear to ear.

ROSINA: Let me go!!!!!

LEONE: Where's Silia? I don't want her to see this.

MAMA: *(Fighting),* Get a priest! Get a priest!

(Bells continue.)

(End of Scene Nine)

Scene Ten
DISTANT BELLS

(Field near train tracks—same as Scene One. The church bells in the distance. LUCIO *[of Scene One] leans against a stick and smokes.)*

(Pause)

(Suddenly a woman's groan off. LUCIO *flinches, smokes. A train whistle in the distance.)*

*(*SILIA *enters. She is trembling, white.)*

SILIA: It's coming. I hear it.

*(*LUCIO *nods.)*

SILIA: Does it usually slow down?

LUCIO: Sometimes. Sometimes it doesn't.

SILIA: I'll take my chances.

(Train getting closer)

SILIA: Here. Thank you.

(Hands LUCIO *the wire she's been holding)*

SILIA: It's in the ditch. Could you bury it?

(Without looking at her, he nods.)

SILIA: I wonder what the bells are for? *(Short pause)* Goodbye.
Tell my parents, will you? It won't be hard.

(Train closer)

SILIA: I better go to the tracks. *(She looks back.)*

LUCIO: Silia?

SILIA: Yes?

LUCIO: Why?

SILIA: Because American millionaires like their women skinny.

(Train loud)

(She runs.)

SILIA: Slow down! Slow down!

(She's off.)

(Train noise very loud)

(End of Scene Ten)

Scene Eleven
WEEKS LATER

(On a train. PINOCCHIO *and an American* SOLDIER *in uniform, who reads a book.)*

PINOCCHIO: What are you reading?

SOLDIER: What?

PINOCCHIO: I asked what you're reading.

SOLDIER: A book.

(PINOCCHIO *makes a face.)*

PINOCCHIO: I know that, what kind of book. A mystery?

SOLDIER: Yes. A mystery. *(Goes back to his reading)*

PINOCCHIO: I thought so. You Americans are always reading mysteries. Is there a private eye?

SOLDIER: A what?

PINOCCHIO: Is there a private eye? In the mystery?

SOLDIER: I haven't gotten to the murder yet, so how should I know if there's a private eye?

(Pause)

PINOCCHIO: It usually says on the back if there is.

SOLDIER: *(Looks at him)* I didn't read the back. *(Reads)*

PINOCCHIO: Oh. *(Short pause)* Do you mind if I read the back?

SOLDIER: Yes.

PINOCCHIO: Oh. *(Pause)* Are you a real American?

SOLDIER: Look, buster, what do you want to say?

PINOCCHIO: I only ask because Americans are usually so open. You ask them a question and they spill out their whole lives. Americans wear their hearts on their sleeves.

SOLDIER: I'm an American. *(Reads)*

PINOCCHIO: Ever been to Italy?

SOLDIER: North Africa.

PINOCCHIO: I was just in Italy. Actually, I come from Italy. So it was sort of like going home. My father's dead. But it's a small village so I had lots of people to see. Italians love Americans. They look to America. I couldn't tell them enough about America. Their curiosity was inexhaustible. That's nice to see. I mean, because you hear so many stories. How they hate Americans. And some of that's there all right. Course, they all think we're millionaires. They got a lot of fantasies like that about America. They may love us, but they sure don't understand us. And that's why they're always trying to take advantage. What they don't realize is that we may be very open people, you understand, that we really want to be good and do good and all that, but it doesn't mean we're pushovers. It's like with a child, you spoil them and they'll end up rotten. You got to be tough with them—it's for their own good. They got to stand on their own two feet sometime, so they better start learning soon. Don't you think? *(Short pause)* I mean, America can't do everything. Even if we could, they'd still just end up resenting us. You know what I think?

SOLDIER: Tell me.

PINOCCHIO: I think that the best thing we can give those people—and those people are my people, or they once were my people, because that's where my roots are and roots are important, we often forget that because we're such a mobile population, but they are important and that's why it's important to keep those ties, even if it's just writing back and telling the folks how well you're doing—they take pride in that, it gives them something to talk about. But anyway, I was saying what we should give these people—it's not food or clothes or new technologies, that's not what they really need—what they need is an American spirit. We got to teach them what we know almost instinctively from birth, and that's that if you want to do something, you can. It's all up to you. The only thing that's standing in your way is yourself. That's what they got to learn. And that's something positive. And that's why the Reds don't have an iceberg's chance in hell against us Americans. Because we are teaching something positive, and everything they're teaching is negative. We tell people to hope and they're telling people to give up. They are telling people to quit, and people—in my experience—don't like quitters. No. And they never will. *(Short pause)* We're a super power now; we got the bomb, we can do whatever we want in the world. We can take over the whole world if we wanted to. But we don't want to—and that says about all that needs to be said about America. All we want is for people to be free. Like us. So we get kicked in the teeth sometimes. That's sometimes the cost of trying to help people. But that's not going to make us run away from our responsibilities. Everybody's looking toward America. The eyes of the world are upon us. Everybody's asking themselves—what kind of people are these new giants? That's why we got to show them we won't take any shit, and once they see that, the better off we'll all be. *(Short pause)* We're slowing down. *(Short pause)* Can you read the station sign?

SOLDIER: Iowa City.

PINOCCHIO: Iowa City. Look at those fields. This country is so big. It takes your breath away. A man can do as he wants here. *(Pause)* How's the book?

SOLDIER: It's getting better. *(Short pause)* I got to the murder.

(Pause)

END OF PLAY

THE VIENNA NOTES

THE VIENNA NOTES was produced by Playwrights Horizons (André Bishop, Artistic Director, Robert Moss, Producing Director) on 18 January 1979. The cast and creative contributors were:

STUBBS . . . . Dan Desmond
RIVERS . . . . Kate McGregor-Stewart
GEORGIA . . . . Marcell Rosenblatt
GUNTER . . . . Richard Bey

Director . . . . André Ernotte
Set designer . . . . Heidi Landesman
Costume designer . . . . William Ivey Long
Lighting designer . . . . Paul Gallo
Special effects . . . . Jack Stewart
Sound designers . . . . David Rapkin

THE VIENNA NOTES was first presented in workshop at Guthrie II, directed by Bruce Siddons.

CHARACTERS & SETTING

STUBBS, *a politician*
RIVERS, *his secretary*
GEORGIA
GUNTER, *a porter*

An intimate hotel in Vienna and a country house outside Vienna.

Scene One

(Setting: Vienna. The sitting room of a suite in an old and intimate hotel.)

(Upstage center, a handsome antique writing desk faces the audience.)

(Left, a red velvet divan, laced with fringe, a potted fern, and two small tables, one with a lamp, the other with a black telephone.)

(Door to the hallway, right.)

(Stage dark. Lights fade up.)

(Pause)

(The door is opened. GEORGIA, STUBBS, RIVERS, *and finally* GUNTER *enter.* GEORGIA *(early thirties) is well and fashionably dressed. (She is the Chairwoman of the Lecture Committee for the Vienna Americans' Club.)* STUBBS *(fifties) wears a nicely fitting overcoat and a Russian-style fur hat. (He is a U S Senator).* RIVERS *(late forties) wears a cloth coat, not very stylish. (She is* STUBBS' *secretary.)* GUNTER *is the porter and he carries in the suitcases.)*

GEORGIA: *(Entering)* Well? What did I tell you? Just what did I tell you? Was I right? Or was I right?

(She looks for a reaction but gets none. STUBBS *has begun to take off his coat, loosen his tie, etc, all the while taking in the room.* RIVERS *just stands for the moment and looks around.)*

GEORGIA: It's everything I said it was, isn't it? *(She looks for a reaction, but gets none.)* And you can't believe your eyes, can you? *(No response)* Vienna! City of mystery. City of ambiance. City of Mozart. City with that Old World charm. That musty charm. You can just breathe it. Breathe it!

RIVERS: *(Who wasn't listening)* What?

GEORGIA: Breathe!

*(*RIVERS *breathes.)*

GEORGIA: Vienna! City of intrigue. City of cafes. City of wine. Of singing. Of glittering chandeliers. And it's all right here before us. All of it. The best part. You can just see it all right here. And feel it. Go 'head! *(No response; short pause)* And that lace. Just look at that lace. And that velvet. Incredible. And look at the craftsmanship in that desk. Do you believe that? Do you believe that! *(Short pause; no reaction)* Well, I can't. I've lived here almost two years and I still can't. I mean, you don't find three hundred-year-old rooms like this in America, unless they're carved into the side of a cliff. Am I right? Or am I right?

RIVERS: *(Taking off her coat; not really paying attention)* You're right.

GEORGIA: I knew you'd say that. I just knew it. Because you know why? Because that's exactly how I felt. I felt the same way. When Winslow and I arrived here. *(Smiles to herself; almost laughs)* Boy, do I remember that.

(As she continues talking, she opens her purse and looks for a handkerchief. But before she finds one, she has to first take out a few items—a compact, an address book, and a snub-nosed revolver. RIVERS *notices but is not terribly surprised.)*

GEORGIA: Brother. Did you know I was disappointed at first? It's true. I was. My first glance. We got off the plane and God only knows what I was expecting to find. But it certainly wasn't just another airport. An ordinary old airport. Winslow says my face dropped a good foot. And I'll bet it did. 'Cause all I was thinking, see, was: Georgia, girl, you could be anywhere. This is just an airport. I thought that. Admittedly, the jet lag didn't help. But I. I'll admit it. On first glance I was terribly disappointed. Isn't that crazy? *(She looks around and realizes no one is listening.)* Gunter, take the bags into the bedrooms.

STUBBS: *(Who has been looking over some scraps of paper he had in his pants pocket; without looking up:)* Not the brown one. That oughta stay out here.

*(*GUNTER *leaves the brown bag and exits left with the others.)*

(Pause)

*(*GEORGIA *looks around, waiting for someone to say something.)*

GEORGIA: *(Finally)* And then we took a taxi. A Mercedes. At least that's a difference, I told myself. But the ride, itself. Well, it wasn't much. Was it? It wasn't anything really. Anything to write home about, that is. I mean, the same city sounds, you know. The same sort of smells, you know. The same chuckholes you could find anywhere. Maybe there was a bit more police around. You know, checking cars. That kind of thing. But that isn't something you'd jump for joy about, right? *(Short pause. No reaction.)* So I guess you could say—are you with me?

*(*STUBBS *and* RIVERS *have opened the brown bag and are rummaging through it, taking out notebooks, files, thumbing through these, sorting them out and piling some on the desk.)*

GEORGIA: So I guess you could say. That by the time we pulled up in front of the hotel. As a matter of fact this same hotel. *(No reaction)* You could say, I wanted to go home. I was nearly in tears. I'd expected something mysterious. Something, you know, Viennese. But all I'd got was, well, you know. And then we got into the lift. And I remember feeling so tired and so resentful, but thinking in utter disbelief, mind you, that

Winslow—and that meant me too—that Winslow had a contract to stay put here for three years. Three whole years! Do you believe that? *(No reaction, feeling more and more self-conscious)* And so on that note. I remember this so well. Listen. We walked into our room. It wasn't this room. But the effect is the same. And I saw the antiques. And my mouth opened. And I saw the fringe on the lamps. And I got a lump in my throat. I felt the velvet. And it was velvet. And all of a sudden. I found myself shaking. I was shaking. I was! I found myself almost spellbound. I had to pinch myself. Pinch, I said! Pinch! And I turned to Winslow. And tears began to roll down my cheeks. I stretched out my arms. This is wonderful, I wanted to say. But the words wouldn't come out. But I guess he knew what I was thinking. Because he smiled. And I remember laughing. Just laughing, you know, as the tears, they just streamed down my face.

(STUBBS *has unplugged the lamp on the table and has taken it over to the desk.)*

STUBBS: *(To* RIVERS*)* You see a socket?

RIVERS: *(Still going through the bag)* There's gotta be one somewhere around the desk, Stubbs.

(Pause)

(GEORGIA, *now very self-conscious, very confused, tries to get a hold of herself. She goes to* RIVERS *and taps her on the shoulder.* RIVERS *looks up.)*

GEORGIA: So you like it? The room, I mean.

RIVERS: *(Looks around)* It's nice. *(Returns to the bag)*

GEORGIA: You mean that?

STUBBS: I can't find one.

RIVERS: Just a sec. I'll look.

(RIVERS *goes to the desk, leaving* GEORGIA *alone.)*

GEORGIA: I knew you would. I knew you'd like it. So I guess all the trouble I went through was worth it, right? *(No response)* With my club, I mean. In talking it out. In coming to an agreement. There's a lot that had to be taken into account. It wasn't all that easy. Believe me. A lot. In choosing a hotel for a guest speaker. Especially for a Senator. Especially for a Senator who'd been a whisker away, right, from being a President. There's a whole lot. Isn't there?

RIVERS: Here's a socket that cord would reach.

(STUBBS *unravels the cord, plugs it in.)*

GEORGIA: But do you know what finally made us decide? On this hotel? It was something *I* said. Do you want to hear?

*(*RIVERS *returns to the bar.)*

GEORGIA: Do you really? I said. Listen to this. I said, if he is going to visit Vienna. If Senator Stubbs is going to be our guest in Vienna. Then, damn it, he should visit Vienna. Do you see what I meant?

(No response: STUBBS *at the desk, looking through papers)*

GEORGIA: You do? *(No response)* Well, was I right? *(No response)* Or was I right? *(No response. She is upset, though making a great effort to control herself.)*

STUBBS: *(Without looking up)* I got a few notes in my coat, Rivers.

RIVERS: I'll get 'em. *(She does.)*

(Pause)

*(*GEORGIA *doesn't know what to do.* GUNTER, *who returned a few moments ago, has been standing left, waiting.)*

GUNTER: *(To* GEORGIA*)* Now?

GEORGIA: *(Almost yells:)* What?! Oh, right. I'm sorry. I nearly forgot. Sure, Gunter. Go ahead and tell your story. God knows, maybe they'll be interested in that.

*(*GEORGIA *sits on the divan:* GUNTER *moves center, clears his throat. Every so often,* STUBBS *and* RIVERS *pick up their heads for a second and listen to* GUNTER, *but for most of the time they ignore him and continue what they've been doing.)*

GUNTER: It was a winter's evening, one hundred and twenty years ago tonight. The crowd lining Kartnerstrasse was three deep as Franz Josef's white carriage rattled along. Peasants in red scarves cheered. The gypsies rang bells. Others waved and bowed. The wheels of the carriage made a clapping sound over the cobble stone. And the breath of the horses created small clouds in the air.

At the Opera House, the carriage door was opened by an attendant dressed in gold. He held his hat and bowed. All in one movement. And the Emperor walked out. "Oh!" gasped the crowd. Then absolute silence, except for the scraping noise of Franz Josef's sword against the Opera steps. The mammoth wooden doors opened seemingly by themselves, and the Emperor slightly tilted his head to acknowledge the crowd. Which then went wild.

Once inside, the Emperor took his royal box. The opera that evening was FAUST. Ambassadors stood and raised their plumed hats to the box. Women hid their faces, though not their eyes. The orchestra stood and saluted the salute they had practiced earlier that day. And then the overture began. And the music sounded heavenly.

While Faust was singing his doubts, Franz Josef scanned the audience with a pair of opera glasses. They had been a gift from the Dutch Ambassador. In return, the Emperor had given Holland a very fine harpsichordist. Everyone was satisfied. The conductor was nervous, and drops of perspiration formed like beads on the top of his bald head. And Faust sang his heart out.

Suddenly, a woman, not in a box, but in the loge, caught the Emperor's eye. He twitched. He felt his stomach tighten. He examined her closely through the glasses. He could not take his eyes off her. Franz Josef consulted with his ministers. But no one knew her name. Ushers went scurrying to other boxes. The French Ambassador thought she might be French. The Opera House was filled with whispers. Even the singer playing Mephistopheles glanced her way. Finally, the curtain for the interval came down.

Attendants rushed to the woman's seat. But only to find her gone. Hallways were quickly searched. Carriages which lined the streets were examined. Franz Josef was beside himself. "Find her!" he yelled. And ministers hid behind each other. Then, just as the Emperor was about to give up hope, a small young man brought to him a white glove. It had been left under her seat, he said. And the Emperor handed the man a coin. Franz Josef held the glove loose in his hand. He tried to smell it. He held it up to the light. He played with it as if it were alive. Then. A card fell out. Franz Josef screamed at his ministers to stand back. There was an address on the card.

Franz Josef gave his driver the address. The horses were whipped. The carriage lurched back. A beggar was nearly run over. "Faster!" shouted the Emperor. "Faster!" he continued to shout, until the driver had finally replied, "We're here."

And so Franz Josef found himself standing before this very hotel. My great great grandfather almost fainted as he bowed. The Emperor took two stairs at once. He appeared almost to fly. His heart obviously was racing. He found the door without much trouble. He checked the number with that on the card a third, and then a fourth time. It matched. It matched. He smelled the glove which he still held loose in his hand. And then. Then he pounded. He pounded harder. And the door creaked as it opened. And Franz Josef, Emperor of the Austrian- Hungarian Empire, was heard to sigh. And the door swiftly closed behind him. *(Short pause)* Three hours later, the Emperor left this hotel.

(Pause.)

*(*GUNTER *exits right.)*

*(*GEORGIA *waits for a reaction.)*

GEORGIA: *(Finally:)* Well? *(No response)* Isn't that incredible? Can you believe that? Doesn't it just make your skin crawl? *(No response)* See, it was this hotel. This same hotel. Right here. That happened right here!! *(No response; she explodes.)* GOD DAMN IT! HERE!! HERE!! WILL YOU PAY ATTENTION!! HE DOESN'T TELL THAT TO EVERYONE!!! THAT

WAS SPECIAL!! THAT WAS SUPPOSED TO BE A TREAT!!! I PAID HIM TWENTY BUCKS TO DO THAT!!! LISTEN!!! LISTEN!!!

*(*RIVERS *looks up.* STUBBS *has "snuck" a glance but keeps writing in a notebook.* GEORGIA *tries to calm herself, to put on a "better face".)*

GEORGIA: I'm sorry. I don't know what got into me. Did I tell you how much I've looked forward to this? I have. Really. Meeting you? Greeting you? I must have imagined, you know. In the mirror. Before falling asleep. I must have imagined a thousand times what I'd say to you. To make you comfortable. To get you to enjoy yourself. Give you a good time. But I never really imagined. Not this. *(Short pause; erupts again)* LOOK! I'VE GONE TO A FUCKING LOT OF TROUBLE FOR YOU!!

*(*STUBBS *and* RIVERS *watch; short pause; then nearly out of control:)*

GEORGIA: Look. I may be a nobody. Okay. Georgia nobody. Granted. Fine. I will buy that. But it seems to me. It just seems to me. Am I wrong? Tell me if I'm wrong. But it just seems to me that that don't mean you couldn't have. You couldn't have. Well, does it? DOES IT!! *(No response)* DOES IT!!!! Okay, Jesus, maybe I'm not the smartest. Maybe I'm no big shot. But you could have. DAMN IT, YES YOU COULD HAVE PRETENDED!!! *(Pause. She goes to the door, opens it, looks back, no response. She exits, slamming the door.)*

RIVERS: We'll see you tonight then? Nine-thirty, wasn't it? *(She returns to her work.)*

GEORGIA: *(Quickly reentering; hopeful:)* What? What did you say? *(No response)* Were you talking to me? *(No response. She turns slowly, defeated, and exits, closing the door gently this time.)*

(Pause)

*(*STUBBS *remains staring at the door, obviously thinking.)*

RIVERS: *(Notices he isn't working)* What's the matter, Stubbs?

STUBBS: Oh, boy.

RIVERS: Hey, I thought you couldn't wait to knock off this entry? Come on. *(Short pause)* What's wrong with you? You said you couldn't concentrate on the plane so as soon as we could get set. Well, we're just about set. Stubbs, we're set.

(Finally notices he's thinking, has that look which she has seen so many times before)

RIVERS: Oh. I get you. I think I'm with you. But when the hell did that happen? When did you get another one? About the girl? Is it about the girl?

STUBBS: Maybe. We'll just have to see, won't we? See if it plays.

RIVERS: Then you want me to get ready to write?

STUBBS: What? Yeh. That's a good idea. Get yourself ready. 'Cause this kinda thing you gotta get while it's hot.'Cause it's gonna be all detail. All in tiny bits. Now sit on the couch and give me some room for this. Some breathing space. *(Still staring)* Okay. Okay. It might just be nice. You got a notebook?

RIVERS: I had to get a new one. The last was about full.

STUBBS: So what's the number?

RIVERS: The last was eighty-three.

STUBBS: *(Still staring)* So then it's notebook number eighty four. Put it down.

*(*RIVERS *writes.)*

STUBBS: "The Memoirs of Henry Stubbs, United States Senator." Put in the date.

RIVERS: *(Writes)* Done.

STUBBS: *(Still staring)* Good. Very good.

(Suddenly he breaks his stare and begins getting into what he says; RIVERS *writes.)*

STUBBS: My hotel suite. Vienna. I had just flown in from the U S. Still with that taste. That stale airplane taste in my mouth. Uncomfortable. With aching legs. Feeling tired. Weak. Not quite all there. Not quite solid. The jet-sound still inside me. Still echoing. Drumming. Pulsing. So, feeling first, that I had better get down to work. And second, that I wanted to stretch out. Relax. Maybe a hot bath would be nice.

So as I walked in. Off went the coat. The tie was loosened. The file case unpacked. A place of work set up. To get cracking. To get to the point where I wouldn't feel guilty about stretching out. And unwinding. And taking it slow and easy. So all this while I looked around. Took things in. Not bad, I thought. This suite. Got a certain. *Je ne sais quoi.* A feeling to it. A certain charm. That I like. That pleased me.

So all this while my hostess. From the Americans' Club. Where I'm to deliver a lecture tonight. *(Quickly turns to* RIVERS*, snaps his fingers)* Name!

RIVERS: *(Writing)* Georgia.

STUBBS: *(Continuing)* By the name of Georgia. So all this while I heard her talk. About this and that. About Vienna this. Mozart that. Even something about Mercedes. I heard only fragments as they cracked my concentration. I heard only the strain. The tone of the voice. And this, for an instant, concerned me. Something odd. Something out of whack. It nicked me. I rubbed my eyes. I wondered, what kind of talk is...? But before I could finish the thought, the voice became silent. Still. And the porter... *(Turns to* RIVERS*)* The porter?

*(*RIVERS *nods.)*

STUBBS: He took over for a while.

So there was a calm. In retrospect, I would probably say, a calm before the storm. But then, there was just a calm, in which I turned back to my work. Back to the desk. Back to my fingers, which I watched move silently across the piece of paper. Back to urging myself. Telling myself, concentrate. Concentrate. And "hot bath".

But soon. How long? I'd lost touch. Lost a feel for the time. Like maybe a rash one first feels before it turns red. Just a hint. Just an itch. I felt this sudden. This growing sensation. Tension. Around me. In the room. It seemed to be pressing up against me. Nudging me. It seemed to have somehow changed the complexion. Of the air. The atmosphere here. Blurring it. Confusing it. Just a general fuzzy sensation that something was about to. On the very verge of. What is going...?

But before I could even get the words into my brain. The sensation, it was past that point. Past the point of dealing with. Way the hell past. Because this woman's voice. It was back. Like gangbusters. This Georgia. I was hearing her now shout: "GOD DAMN IT! GOD DAMN IT!" So what I'd felt to be growing like an itch, was now, well now it was building. It was crescendoing. Her words, gaining speed. Faster. What is she...? FASTER! Too god damn fast. Getting run together. Sounding to my ears more like emotions now. More like tiny little screams: "ATTENTION!!" "SPECIAL!!" "FUCKING TROUBLE!!"

I listened. I craned my ears. If that's possible. If that is feasible. But no sense. Found nonsense. So I'm just telling myself, these things; these annoyances. These obnoxious annoyances. They happen. They can't be. No help. They just come with the position. Of being powerful. Of being well known. So what is the use. What's the. Just gotta tolerate it, that's all. Just gotta live with this, sort of. TOLERATE!! I scream at myself. And I jam my finger into the paper, trying to doodle a circle. What can I do? So I draw a crowd. So people stare at me. So I'm just shown to my hotel suite and a woman. This woman, she is screaming: "I'M NOBODY!!" SO WHAT THE HELL CAN I DO?!!! THAT'S YOUR PROBLEM!! I want to scream. I want to shove my face at her and scream.

And then. As I am shaking my head and thinking, not much more. There's not much more of this I can take. Well, she is just hitting her stride. What had come before. What had come out before sounding like a last-breath effort. Well now, now, it sounds like an offhand comment compared to. With this. "THAT DOES IT!!!" I'm thinking the same thing. "THAT DOES IT!!" Then: "DAMN IT!!" Then: "YOU COULD HAVE!" I'm biting my lip. BITE! Then: "YOU COULD HAVE!!!" I'm rubbing my face. I'm thinking: hold back. Hold back. Then, finally: "YOU COULD HAVE PRETENDED!!!!" *(Short pause)*

Then calm. A couple of heart beats. What next? I loosen my grip and drop my pen. Like a pin dropped. That quiet. Then. BANG!! And I jump as the door was slammed shut. And I'm thinking. Boy, am I thinking: "hot bath. Hot bath. Hot bath."

(Short pause. RIVERS *writes.* STUBBS, *out of breath, though suddenly now businesslike, out of the story)*

STUBBS: Okay. That's it. Not bad. Not half bad. Maybe a little rough in spots. But what the hell. We can fix that. *(To* RIVERS*)* Mark my thoughts for italics.

RIVERS: Right.

STUBBS: Maybe a bit slow here and there. Can't tell yet. It felt okay. Not wonderful. But okay. *(To* RIVERS*)* You done?

RIVERS: *(Writing)* Just about.

STUBBS: Well, check *her* words. Make sure you have 'em all in quotes. I don't want any confusion 'bout who the hell said what.

RIVERS: I always check, Stubbs.

STUBBS: The opening. Definitely. The opening was sluggish. I could feel that. I remember feeling just that. Loose. Very loose. "I did this. I did that." I mean, Jesus, if people are really gonna get this into. I mean, go through it themselves. If they're gonna be empathizing themselves blue. If they're really gonna get the picture of the kind of stuff I go through. Or, depending. Depending on when the hell they read this, of the kind of stuff I went through in my life. Then, Christ. Playing loose. Playing loose, especially early. That won't do. You gotta let 'em in. And let 'em in fast.

RIVERS: Done.

STUBBS: What? Oh great. Let me see that. Who knows, maybe I'm wrong. Maybe I'm wrong and it just seemed loose at the time.

*(*STUBBS *looks over the notebook. The door opens.* GEORGIA *enters with great hesitation.)*

GEORGIA: I. I got halfway home. And I. Well I suddenly remembered that I'd forgot to tell you.

*(*RIVERS *looks at her;* STUBBS *ignores or doesn't really hear her.)*

GEORGIA: You won't say no, will you? It's not that far. Just a few kilometers. *(Short pause)* Winslow's home getting ready. *(Short pause)* If you're worried about getting back. If that's it. Well, you shouldn't. That shouldn't be a problem. *(Short pause)* You really won't say no, will you? *(Short pause)* But if you'd rather not.... It you have other plans. *(Short pause)* If you're tired. *(Short pause)* If you want to be alone. *(Short pause)* If you would really rather not.

RIVERS: Rather not what, Georgia?

GEORGIA: Uh. Come to *my* house. For dinner.

RIVERS: Well, Stubbs?

STUBBS: *(Looking at the notebook. Suddenly:)* GOD DAMN IT!!!

(Looks up, notices both RIVERS *and* GEORGIA *are looking at him)*

STUBBS: It is sluggish. *(Short pause)* Well, what? I wasn't listening.

(Blackout)

Scene Two

(Setting: GEORGIA *and Winslow's rented converted farmhouse. The living room.)*

(Upstage left and angled center—door, paned windows with drapes on either side of the door. This on a platform, so there is a step down to the living room proper.)

(Center: sofa, table with vase, wooden bench, coffee table, telephone, oriental rug, etc.)

(Stage dark. Lights up)

(Door opens. GEORGIA, RIVERS, *and then* STUBBS *enter.* RIVERS *writes in her notebook.* GEORGIA *listens fascinated.)*

STUBBS: *(Entering; he is "into" his story, feeling almost everything he says.)* And the hum. Drone. Soothed me. Almost massaged. For moments, I felt myself almost encased by the sound. Like in a bubble. Like in a cell. And the lights, they jarred. First, the street lamps. While still driving through the city. Then the oncoming cars. Their lights flickered quickly across my face. It felt almost like I was blinking.

GEORGIA: *(Taking off her coat; quietly, to* RIVERS:*)* He said, this is for his memoirs?

RIVERS: *(Writing)* Sh-sh.

GEORGIA: I'm sorry.

STUBBS: *(Continuing)* So I closed my eyes. An effort. The window had been rolled down. I stuck my face. Almost shoved it. Into the rush of night air. At first, the urge. The impulse to hold my hair. Keep it out of my eyes. But eventually. Finally. I let it blow. There was conversation in the front seat. That much I knew. But just "conversation". Because the wind. The drone. All combined. It sounded like a foreign language.

GEORGIA: This is exciting. *(Loud whisper)* Winslow! Come and hear this!

STUBBS: A reach for a cigarette. The explosion of the match. The glow. I felt down the side of the door. Where's the ashtray? Georgia had to tell me where it was. I can find it, I thought. I CAN FIND IT!!!

GEORGIA: *(To* RIVERS; *trying to be quiet)* He's gonna use that? What *I* said?

STUBBS: I felt old. My hand on the leather seat. Never that smooth. My skin was never that smooth. I looked around me. The blue dashboard light. The red glow. The oncoming cars. A landscape. A landscape of dreams.

GEORGIA: Could you hold it a minute. Just until I got Winslow. You couldn't imagine what a thrill he'd get. *(She exits left.)*

STUBBS: And then I saw myself. Don't be sentimental, I wanted to say. Don't be indulgent. But I saw myself like this. Like here. Other cars. In other back seats. Other cities. Countries. Drivers. All blurred. All stuck together. I wanted to reach into my brain and pull them apart. I saw a Spaniard with medals pinned to his chest. The two of us. Back seat. But where? Then I saw papers. Briefs for 'eyes only'. Piled across my lap. My head buried. My head hidden. Now I'm alone. And now police cars both front and back. Where is... And now there. THERE! DID YOU FEEL THAT?!! That was the thump as we drove across a median. Because this is urgent. See, this. Essential. This. What is this?

GEORGIA: *(Off)* Winslow!

STUBBS: And now my arms. Outstretched. The top down. And a beauty queen both left and. And right. And we're smiling. We're. This a parade of. Marking what? For what...? But the sunshine I can definitely feel the... But now it's blurred. Now it is in the middle of the. It's pitch. It's. I can't see a thing. Just my driver. We're waiting for. This, an Army airstrip. We're waiting for an important. For some. And he and I. We're ol' buddies. We are. We're shooting the bull. Talking good ol'. Football. And smoking. We were smoking. We were.

GEORGIA: *(Off)* Winslow!

STUBBS: Then I coughed. As I rubbed out my cigarette. And I could feel the veins. The forehead veins. Pulse blood. Straining. Knew my face, now beet. Now bright red. And my chest. My chest, it aches. And I rubbed at my brain. Almost. Wanted to. Nearly kneaded it. Until I could finally. Just close my eyes. Shut them. Without it hurting.

GEORGIA: *(Entering; concerned)* I even looked on the porch.

(She exits right, to check out the bedrooms)

STUBBS: *(After a brief pause)* And when I finally woke. Because the light overhead had come on. Because Rivers' voice, I heard it now, was outside the car. She's out there tapping on the window and saying. What's she saying. That I'm old? That I'm feeble? That I get things sometimes mixed up? Is she saying where we...? What city? What country? What's she telling me? What am I supposed to know that she's telling me! Speak up! Rivers, speak up! WHAT!! WHAT!! TELL ME!! TELL ME!! I DON'T KNOW WHERE I AM!!! *(Pause)* But Rivers. When I finally can make it. Understand. All she is saying. She's just saying, "We're here."

(Short pause. STUBBS *suddenly breaks out of the story.)*

STUBBS: That's it. What did you do with my cigarettes?

RIVERS: *(Writing)* You had 'em in the car, Stubbs. You want me to check?

STUBBS: You got that down?

RIVERS: *(Writing)* I will in a minute.

STUBBS: Then you finish. I'll go hunt them up.

GEORGIA: *(Off)* Winslow!

*(*STUBBS *opens the door, then turns back to* RIVERS.*)*

STUBBS: What did you think? It wasn't what you'd call loud. Not in fucking neon. But the old guy just remembering. There's a built-in thing in that. The situation itself, I would think, oughta be enough to grab 'em and hold them in. Don't you?

RIVERS: *(Writing; sincerely:)* It was nice, Stubbs. Really. Just real nice.

STUBBS: Good. You know, it was just so easy, you begin to get doubts.

RIVERS: Well, you shouldn't.

STUBBS: Thanks. *(Turns to exit, stops)* Who the hell is that?

RIVERS: *(Writing)* Somebody out there?

GEORGIA: Winslow! *(Off)*

RIVERS: *(Writing)* Must be her Winslow. *(Calling:)* He's outside!!

STUBBS: *(Looking out)* Boy, what a fucked-up place this is. I heard it was bad, but shit. Look at that, Rivers. You gotta carry a gun just to go outside your own house. That's somethin'.

RIVERS: *(Writing)* He's got a gun?

STUBBS: Which one is Winslow?

RIVERS: *(Stops writing, looks up)* Which *one*?

STUBBS: Yeh, there's at least... And what the hell do they have on their faces?

(Suddenly, off, GEORGIA *screams at the top of her lungs.)*

*(*RIVERS *sets the notebook down.)*

STUBBS: What is wrong with her? *(Returns to looking out the door)* It looks like... They're in a shadow. I'll be able to tell when they get closer.

*(*RIVERS *looks toward where* GEORGIA *screamed from then back at* STUBBS*—something frightening begins to dawn on her.)*

RIVERS: *(Forced calm)* Stubbs. Close the door.

STUBBS: Huh?

RIVERS: Just close it.

(STUBBS, confused, does so.)

RIVERS: *(Screams:)* NOW BOLT IT!!

STUBBS: What are you talking about?

(GEORGIA enters, in shock, blood stains on her hands and dress.)

RIVERS: *(Seeing her)* Oh, my God! OH NO!! NO!!!!

GEORGIA: *(Screams:)* THEY KILLED HIM!!!!!

RIVERS: Please, Stubbs. PLEASE BOLT THE FUCKING DOOR!!

(Very confused, STUBBS bolts the door and moves in front of the window.)

RIVERS: A gun. where's a gun? A GUN!! Think. Think. Okay. That's right. I saw one in her purse. Now where's her purse? *(Sees STUBBS at the window)* Stubbs, get away from the window.

(He doesn't move.)

RIVERS: Where's the purse? *(To GEORGIA)* WHERE'S YOUR GOD DAMN PURSE!!!

(GEORGIA moves her hand.)

RIVERS: Over there? Over where? I don't see it. Stubbs, do you see it? WHERE OVER THERE!!!

STUBBS: *(Confused, but calm)* It's on the couch. You want me to get it for you?

RIVERS: *(Seeing that STUBBS has not moved)* I WANT YOU TO GET DOWN!!!

STUBBS: Okay. *(Starts to stoop)*

RIVERS: DOWN!!!!!

(STUBBS ducks down.)

(Gun shot off, the window over STUBBS shatters.)

(He freezes.)

(GEORGIA screams.)

(RIVERS has found the revolver, runs to the window, ducking down, raises the gun over her head.)

RIVERS: *(Running to the windows)* DON'T COME ANY CLOSER!! DON'T COME ANY CLOSER!! *(She shoots four times:)* STOP! STOP! STOP! STOP!!!! *(Then she freezes, out of breath.)*

(Pause)

STUBBS: *(Picks up his head. peaks out the window)* They're gone. Or at least they're out of sight. *(He closes the curtain: to* RIVERS*)* They had ski masks on, didn't they?

GEORGIA: *(Screams:)* WINSLOW!!!!!!!!!!

(Everyone is still.)

(Long pause)

(Slowly, very slowly, STUBBS *and* RIVERS *relax, breathe easier. They get themselves together.* GEORGIA, *in shock, does not move.)*

STUBBS: *(Brushing himself off)* Not bad. Not bad at all. *(Short pause)* But not perfect. *(Short pause)* I know what could have been a lot better.

RIVERS: What do you mean, Stubbs?

STUBBS: What do I mean? I mean her.

(Nods toward GEORGIA.*)*

*(*RIVERS *is confused.)*

STUBBS: I mean when we've got a situation thrown at us like we had here. Just had thrown at us. Well...her just coming in here and screaming her lungs out. Well, that doesn't add much, does it?

RIVERS: I'm still not following, Stubbs.

*(*GEORGIA *watches with growing disbelief.)*

STUBBS: Well, what I'm suggesting is, is that this could have been, well, what it almost was. And that is one of the most interesting. Most exciting. Most dramatic moments of my life. See, it *could have* been. But it wasn't.
Now that doesn't mean it wasn't any good. 'Cause it was. That's obvious. But great? No. No way. 'Cause, see, you don't do great by coming in here and screaming your lungs out. That could work, sure. But it'll work like the shockeroo that it is. Like the stick in the spokes. Like the tack on the chair that it is. Call it what you want. But whatever you call it, it's gonna come out meaning "slick". Meaning "easy". And meaning "cheap". You see what I'm saying now?

RIVERS: Yeh. I think so.

STUBBS: 'Cause, Jesus, where is the build there? In screaming like that. Where's the subtlety? God only knows. I mean, if you're gonna do it right, you gotta pluck it for all that it's worth. Like we did. Like you running around. Like you getting this. Getting that. Like me. "It's all slowly dawning on me." That kind of stuff. That subtle stuff. But screaming? Doing shit but screaming your lungs out? Tell me, where's the build in that?

RIVERS: Yeh. I see what you mean. But what do you think she should have done?

STUBBS: What do I think? Shit. There's a thousand. There are possibilities. By the. There are millions. You really want to know?

(RIVERS *nods.)*

STUBBS: Well. Let me think. She could have. Maybe. Like maybe, she could have come in. You know, without saying anything. No words. Nothing. But maybe holding something. Like. *(Sees the phone book)* Like a book. *(Picks up the phone book)* Okay? Like a book. So she's holding a book. And. I haven't really thought this out. And, she suddenly drops it. *(He drops the book)* And she doesn't pick it up. Doesn't even look down. Like she didn't even know she did anything. So that's odd. That's peculiar. It's obvious something is up, but nothing's been given away. Okay?

RIVERS: Okay.

STUBBS: And then. Maybe she plays with that bracelet. Fasten it. Unfasten it. Her fingers tense. That's how you notice they're shaking. First the bracelet, then the tenseness. Sense of her holding back something. Repressed. Ready to explode. But you don't really know that yet. Just her nervousness, right?

RIVERS: Right.

STUBBS: Then. How about tears down her face. But no sound. No crying. Just the tears. That's very powerful. Very upsetting. And now a comment. She's saying something. One thing. Something off the wall. Something that is definitely gonna register, gonna click a little "uh-oh" in the brain. A little, "What is going on here?" Something like...

RIVERS: "I keep seeing my father's face"?

STUBBS: What? Yeh. That's not bad. And her face blank. No expression whatever. And then she starts to take a step forward. One step. And as if just that little movement brought her back to. Back to her situation. Her hands quickly cover her face. She bends down, trying to remain tough. Remain self-possessed. But can't. Just can't. And then. At that time. Now she can explode. Now. Damn it now, she can scream her lungs out.

RIVERS: Yeh. That's pretty good.

STUBBS: So what do we have. *(He plays "GEORGIA". He drops the book)* The book.

RIVERS: *(Nodding)* The book. Yes.

STUBBS: I don't look down. *(He fiddles with his "bracelet". His hands are shaking.)* No expression on my face.

RIVERS: Right.

STUBBS: "1 keep seeing my father's face."

RIVERS: Good.

STUBBS: And tears. And... *(He starts to take a step. Covers his face, lowers his head slowly and suddenly screams)* Something like that. It *could have* been just great. *(Shakes his head)* You sure you don't have my cigarettes in your purse?

GEORGIA: *(Screams:)* WINSLOW!!!!!

STUBBS: See? See? That's just the kind of thing I've been talking about.

(Blackout)

Scene Three

(Setting: The same)

(Stage dark. Lights fade up.)

*(*RIVERS*, on the couch, holds her notebook.* STUBBS*, near her, standing and thinking.)*

(Pause)

STUBBS: *(To himself)* Okay. Maybe. Then: door. Then: duck. Then: bang. Then: okay. Right.

RIVERS: You ready?

STUBBS: Just a sec. I'm running it over. Then: yeh. And I'm feeling? Right. Uh-huh. I won't be long.

*(*GEORGIA *enters right. She carries a rifle, an automatic revolver, and an ammunition belt. She is still quite "dazed".)*

GEORGIA: *(Entering)* I found these in a closet. *(Holds them up; to* STUBBS*)* Which do you want? The pistol or the rifle?

*(*RIVERS *puts a finger to her lips, to "sh-sh"* GEORGIA.*)*

(Short pause)

GEORGIA: There's also this ammunition belt.

RIVERS: Georgia, not now.

*(*GEORGIA *just looks around, doesn't know what to do.)*

*(*STUBBS*, thinking, sighs.)*

GEORGIA: I'll give you the rifle. *(She sets the rifle and belt on the bench and sits.)*

STUBBS: *(Snaps his fingers)* Okay, Rivers. I think I'm set. So what the hell. Let's give it a go.

RIVERS: *(Set to write)* I'm right with you, Stubbs.

STUBBS: Right. Now just stay with me. *("Envisions" the scenes)* Farmhouse. Country. Outside Vienna. somewhere. God knows where. I didn't. I'm sure

I didn't. I'd just completed an entry. Not bad. Not half bad. Nothing loud. Nothing in neon. And I was thinking, that was easy. That was maybe too easy. So doubts. So concerns. So I was going back over it and thinking and reaching for a cigarette. But the pack's in the car. Rivers tells me. So I was halfway out the door, still fretting, when: who the hell is that? I said, who the hell? Somebody's out there. Oh that must be, Rivers said. Her. Her husband. Okay. So my mind, it moves back a moment. Back a beat. Back to. To maybe it was too god damn easy.

So then. Coming slowly into focus. A gun. Not a whole gun. But the light on the porch reflected itself, say, as a speck on the barrel of the gun. And that appeared to bounce. The speck, that is. As the gun was moved. Boy oh boy, I said. You gotta carry guns in this place. And then. Suddenly, there are three. Not just guns, but men. But not really men. But noses. Their faces, see, were dark. Black. But their noses? Why? They were white. Maybe they, I'm thinking. Maybe wearing what? Mufflers? Beards? I even thought, maybe a native costume. I did. How ridiculous. Do you believe that? See how the mind can play tricks? SEE!!

So three noses. Three specks of light. And there is a scream too. Behind me. From way the hell behind me. And Rivers is saying, close the door. And I'm thinking, but I don't feel much of a breeze. And she's saying, bolt it. And she's screaming, get down. GET DOWN!!!

And so I'm down. Why? I didn't ask. Just did it. No reason. Why the hell argue. But I'll admit to feeling a touch foolish. When: BANG!!! Then: CRASH!!! The two sounds as simultaneous as two sounds can be. Can get. And now I'm covered with glass. A rain of glass, I think. All fast. One one hundredth of a second, maybe. That's all. That is it. The time it took. But I felt it all happen. As in steps. Bang-crash-rain. And I smelled it too. Get this. Don't forget this. The smell of a sudden, almost immediate, discharge of my SWEAT!!!

And my hair, get this. That was the next thing. The next object of my attention. My hair standing up. But, can you believe this. What I noticed. Not head hair. Not neck hair. But the hair on my knuckles. What an odd sensation. What a strange. The knuckles. Of all places. Of all stupid places. Then. Then I look up. And above me. On the sill tottering. One piece. One small jagged piece of glass. On the edge and tottering. That made me shudder. Really. I want to knock it off. I want to push it back. Anything. Either. It's un-nerving. Just as long as it stops tottering on the god damn brink!! I said to myself, something like, "oh no". Not appropriate. Not enough. My hands don't move. Won't budge. Like stumps. Like they had roots. My heart racing. Banging. Like a berserk. Like a berserk something. REACH!? REACH!! DO SOMETHING!! DO SOMETHING!!

(Suddenly, the telephone rings, interrupting the remainder of STUBBS' *entry.)*

*(*STUBBS *and* RIVERS *almost freeze for an instant. Then they turn to* GEORGIA.*)*

(Short pause, as the phone rings.)

GEORGIA: The line was dead just a minute ago.

(Finally. GEORGIA *picks up the phone.* STUBBS *and* RIVERS *watch.)*

GEORGIA: *(Into the phone)* Hello?

RIVERS: *(Quietly. to* STUBBS:*)* Stubbs, do you feel it? The sudden interruption. Everything stops. Then the sense of anticipation. And the mounting tension. Don't you love it?

*(*STUBBS *nods but motions for her to be quiet.)*

GEORGIA: *(To* STUBBS*)* It's them. *(Into the phone)* Yes... Right... I see.... Right... Uh-huh... Uh-huh... Uh-huh... Yes...

RIVERS: *(In a whisper)* There's sort of a built-in suspense 'bout hearing just one side, isn't there? Maybe I should make a note of that. We could use that sometime. What do you think?

*(*STUBBS *nods but again motions for her to be quiet.)*

GEORGIA: *(Into the phone, hiding her face from* STUBBS*)* Yes... Right...
I understand.... We won't try to call.... Right... I will.... I said, I will....
I'll tell the Senator....

(Short pause)

(She hangs up. Can't look STUBBS *or* RIVERS*)*

*(*STUBBS*, scared, begins to slowly back up.)*

STUBBS: *(Finally:)* Tell the Senator what? *(No response)* Tell me what?!

RIVERS: *(Looking through her purse)* All I got is maybe. Maybe eighty dollars at best. The rest's in traveler's checks.

STUBBS: Georgia, please.

RIVERS: And Stubbs has. I'll bet he's got less than I do. But if they want it so bad they can have it. *(She reaches for* STUBBS' *wallet.)*

STUBBS: FORGET THE MONEY!!!

(He pushes RIVERS *away, she falls to the floor.)*

STUBBS: *(To* RIVERS:*)* I'm sorry.

GEORGIA: They want you.

STUBBS: They what?

GEORGIA: They said something about an exchange. How you could be real useful to them. But I didn't really understand much of that. *(Short pause. To* RIVERS*)* They don't want us. We'd be let go.

RIVERS: *(Getting up)* Stubbs, I thought it was a robbery.

GEORGIA: They gave you an hour. I guess, 'cause they know we have guns. They said, maybe if we thought about it for a while we wouldn't do anything dumb.

(STUBBS looks down, he fiddles with his watch.)

GEORGIA: And. And they said one more thing. *(No one looks at her)* They said. They said that killing Winslow. They said that had been a mistake. *(Short pause)* I guess he must have surprised them. Maybe heard them outside or something.

STUBBS: *(Trying to get control of himself, rubs his eyes)* Oh boy.

GEORGIA: What do you think we should do? There's only one neighbor. And they're away for the month. I know, 'cause I'm supposed to be taking in their mail. *(She looks for a response but gets none.)* Except for them, there's nobody within at least a kilometer. *(Short pause)* Did you hear me?

STUBBS: *(Quiet)* What? Just hold it a minute. Just give me a sec to think. Sit down.

(She sits on the bench. Short pause)

GEORGIA: *(Stands)* The milkman's due around six. But that doesn't help, does it?

RIVERS: Sh-sh. Sit down.

(She sits. Short pause)

GEORGIA: *(Stands)* The lecture's in. In less than two hours. Maybe someone'll get concerned enough and drive out here. What do you think?

(RIVERS suddenly and violently grabs GEORGIA and throws her back down. She falls over the bench.)

(For a moment she is dazed, then begins crying.)

GEORGIA: *(Screams:)* WINSLOW, THEY SAID IT WAS A MISTAKE!!!!! *(She cries.)*

(STUBBS suddenly turns to RIVERS and snaps his fingers.)

STUBBS: I'm feeling... I'm feeling angry. Yes! *(He takes a bowl from the table and smashes it on the floor.)*

(GEORGIA shrieks.)

(STUBBS is suddenly calm. He shakes his head. RIVERS crosses out in her notebook what she had just written.)

STUBBS: No. No. That's not what I'm feeling.

(Pause)

(He paces and thinks. GEORGIA confused)

*(*STUBBS *suddenly bellows:)*

STUBBS: THOSE PUNKS!! THOSE GOD DAMN PUNKS!!! *(Suddenly calm)* No. No. I don't feel indignant. Not me. *(Pause. He paces.)*

GEORGIA: *(Quietly:)* Rivers...?

STUBBS: I'm feeling....I'm feeling sentimental. Yes!

(Slowly, with tears almost in his eyes, he approaches RIVERS *and tenderly moves his hand across her cheek. Then he looks down, wipes a tear away, reaches up, and rustles her hair. Then suddenly moves away)*

STUBBS: No. Not even close. *(Pause. He paces and thinks.)*

GEORGIA: Rivers...?

RIVERS: *(Watching* STUBBS*)* What?

GEORGIA: What is he doing, Rivers?

RIVERS: *(Notices that* STUBBS *has stopped pacing)* Sh-sh!

STUBBS: *(Suddenly smiling, arms raised)* I feel happy. I feel full of love! I feel joyous! I do. Yes. I want to wrap my arms around everyone and everything! I do. I do. I feel majestic. Yes. I feel like I've lived a full life. I feel at peace with myself. Yes! I feel.... *(Breaks out of it)* Nope. Nope. I don't feel like that. Nope. Cross it out.

*(*RIVERS *does. Short pause)*

GEORGIA: Rivers...?

STUBBS: *(Quickly)* I see my life passing before my eyes! *(Breaks out)* Uh-uh. No way. Who am I kidding? *(Paces and thinks. Short pause)*

GEORGIA: *(Quietly:)* Rivers, do *you* know what he's doing?

RIVERS: *(Watching* STUBBS*)* Come again?

GEORGIA: I mean, what he is doing, does it make any sense to *you*? *(No response: explodes)* DOES IT?!!!!!

STUBBS: *(Suddenly begins backing toward the door)* I'm alone. And I'm forgotten. I feel small all of a sudden. Small. And unwanted. And unneeded. I feel like a dark speck of something against a white space. *(He is against the door, folding himself, becoming smaller.)* A spec. Just a faint spec. Getting smaller. Dimmer. Fading fast. Going out. Being extinguished!! *(Suddenly shouts:)* HELP ME!!!

*(*GEORGIA *is frightened, starts to scream.)*

*(*STUBBS *breaks out of it. Calm)*

STUBBS: I don't know what to do. There doesn't seem to be a way out.

*(*GEORGIA *shakes her head and mumbles "no".)*

STUBBS: It just don't seem fair. It don't seem to make any sense.
So I'm scared. Yeh.

GEORGIA: No. I don't believe you. No.

(STUBBS sits on the couch.)

GEORGIA: Uh-uh!

RIVERS: Shut up!

GEORGIA: WHY DON'T YOU SHUT UP!!!!!

(Short pause. STUBBS, looks at both RIVERS and GEORGIA. GEORGIA walks to the far end of the room, her back to them.)

STUBBS: *(To RIVERS:)* For a second I thought we had something exciting beginning there. But I guess not. Anyway... *(Sits, "begins":)* I find myself on the couch. Maybe what, three, five minutes since the phone call. Since Georgia had said, her voice dull, her voice somber, "You. They want you."

GEORGIA: *(Without looking at him)* Leave me out of this, please.

STUBBS: Since—"They what?" Me. That's me. So, by now, there has been time for it all to sink in. Yes. To soak through. And I feel afraid.

(GEORGIA laughs.)

STUBBS: I'm scared.

(GEORGIA laughs harder.)

STUBBS: I don't know where to turn....

(GEORGIA laughs)

STUBBS: ...or what to do next!!

(She laughs very hard. RIVERS starts to get up, but STUBBS gestures for her to stay back. He goes to GEORGIA. She continues to laugh as they look at each other. She stops laughing. Pause. He turns away.)

STUBBS: Just who the hell am I trying to kid? She's right. *(He walks away.)*

RIVERS: What???

STUBBS: I mean, what a joke. So—"I'm scared". *(He laughs to himself.)*
If I'm so scared then just what am I doing worrying about. How I'm going to sound to. Look at us, Rivers. I'm telling you, she's right. I can't really be scared.

RIVERS: Stubbs???

STUBBS: It's all this god damn listening and watching and revealing. That's the. My. I mean, how am I supposed to feel. Even a little scared. If all I do is. I mean, enough is. Jesus Christ, why aren't I doing something. About. Instead of hiding behind some lousy memoir that no one will bother to read anyway. Bother to get to know. Bother to love. And what does this say about. The kind of person I. I don't believe me. I don't. I have taken a very simple idea. A hope. An activity say. And I've gone too. It's sick. Isn't it? Isn't it? How could I not care about. With them out. If not about, then at least about me. I'm human after all, aren't I? AREN'T I?!!!!! *(Short pause. He is almost shaking now. Then to himself:)* Stop it. Stop it, Stubbs. *(Quietly to* RIVERS:*)* Don't write that down. I'll get better. I'll be better. *(Suddenly turns on* RIVERS:*)* Will you put that god damn notebook away?!! WILL YOU PUT THAT GOD DAMN NOTEBOOK AWAY?!!!!! *(Pause)* I'll be better. I've got to stop listening to. There's this voice. I can hear it. You can't, I know. It sounds like it's a mile away. I keep wondering, "Mine? Is that mine?" Like in a hollow really. I hear it. Somewhere out there. I mean, in here. It's crying now. It's scared. Afraid. Wailing. And screaming: What are they going to do to me? What are they going to do to me? Help me!! HELP ME!!!!!!! *(He is crying.)*

GEORGIA: He's crying. He's really crying.

(Pause)

STUBBS: *(With tears down his face; to* GEORGIA:*)* Did you like?

*(*GEORGIA *freezes in shock, staggers a few steps back, looks at* STUBBS, *then* RIVERS. *Suddenly, she runs to the door and begins pounding.)*

GEORGIA: *(Pounding and screaming:)* Help me!!! Help me!!!!

(Blackout)

Scene Four

(Setting: The same)

(Stage dark. Lights fade up.)

*(*RIVERS *sits on the couch, going through her notebook, making corrections, additions, etc.* STUBBS *stands behind the couch, he pounds its back, thinking.)*

(Pause)

*(*GEORGIA *enters with a tray—coffee cups, coffee pot, bottle of milk.)*

GEORGIA: I couldn't find the sugar. And I thought it'd just be asking for trouble to turn on the kitchen light to look for it.

(Short pause. She sets tray down on the table in front of RIVERS. STUBBS *goes to the window and peeks out.)*

GEORGIA: I guess I could have pulled the blinds. But I just couldn't face going anywhere near the window. You know what I mean?

RIVERS: *(Without looking up)* What?

(Short pause. STUBBS *returns to behind the couch, continues pounding on its back, thinking.)*

GEORGIA: *(Pouring herself a cup)* It isn't fresh. I just warmed it up. *(Short pause: no response)* We keep the sugar in the counter cabinet. But, you know, when I felt for it, it wasn't there. *(Pours in some milk, picks up her cup)* I guess, I'll have to ask Winslow where he put it.

(Suddenly, RIVERS *looks up at her, and* STUBBS *turns toward her, both waiting for her reaction.* GEORGIA *realizes what she has just said, freezes for an instant, then drops the cup, which shatters.)*

(Short pause as GEORGIA *just stares.)*

STUBBS: *(To* RIVERS:*)* Better. No doubt about it. Much better than screaming her lungs out. She's catching on.

RIVERS: *(Nods)* Very nice, Georgia.

*(*STUBBS *returns to his thinking;* RIVERS *to her notebook.* GEORGIA *sits on the bench and stares.)*

(Pause)

STUBBS: *(Suddenly, without expression)* I feel aggressive. I've been pushed too far. I've taken just about all I'm gonna take. I want to fight.

*(*RIVERS *quickly turns to him. She rifles through the notebook until she finds the first clean page. She gets set to write.)*

STUBBS: Where's the rifle?

RIVERS: *(She tries to write this. Stops. Shakes her pen)* Hold it a second, Stubbs. *(She gets up, goes to her purse.)*

STUBBS: *(At first, not hearing her)* Where's the ri...?!

(Sees RIVERS *is not writing)*

STUBBS: Where are you going? Why aren't you writing?

RIVERS: I'm getting another pen. The other one was running out.

STUBBS: Wait a minute. Tell me something. And what am I supposed to do while you're looking for this pen?

RIVERS: It'll just take a second.

STUBBS: How long it'll take doesn't change the fact that you are holding me up.

RIVERS: I'm sorry, Stubbs.

STUBBS: Sorry for what? Your stupidity? Your incompetence? Your arrogance? Just who the hell do you think you are?

RIVERS: *(Nearly in tears)* It's just that the pen was running...

STUBBS: Look, I don't pay you for excuses. I pay you to write. SO WRITE!!! *(Turns away. Looks around)* NOW, FOR THE LAST TIME, WHERE IS THAT GOD DAMN RIFLE?!!

*(*RIVERS *begins to desperately search her purse.)*

RIVERS: *(Without looking up)* It's next to Georgia.

STUBBS: *(Without moving; to* GEORGIA*)* Give it to me.

(Short pause)

RIVERS: *(Without looking up. To* GEORGIA*)* Give it to him. *(No response; looks up)* Give it to him!!! ...I'll get it, Stubbs.

STUBBS: No! She is going to have to learn just who is in charge here.... Georgia, the rifle. Hand it to me. That's an order.

*(*RIVERS *continues to dig through her purse.)*

*(*GEORGIA *slowly reaches for the rifle, then stops.)*

STUBBS: I said, that is an order.

*(*GEORGIA*, very hesitantly, picks up the rifle and hands it to* STUBBS.*)*

*(*STUBBS *suddenly grabs it away from her; he begins to bounce it in his hands, looking it over, nodding and smiling.)*

RIVERS: *(In a panic)* Stubbs, I can't find another pen.

STUBBS: *(Explodes:)* GOD DAMN IT, WHAT ARE YOU TRYING TO DO TO ME?!! Do I have to do everything myself? You want a pen? *(Yanks one out of his shirt pocket and flings it across the room.)* There's one.... Now shut up and write!!!!

*(*RIVERS *chases after the pen, finds it, and hurries to get set to write.* STUBBS *plays with the gun, trying to get back into the "mood".)*

STUBBS: *("Into" his entry now)* I find a rifle. And for an instant I wait. Expecting. In fact listening for it to somehow bark orders back to me. Into my brain. Back through its barrel. Like Bouganville. With the palm trees. The huts. The steam jackhammers slashing away at the coral. Like my sergeant. Up to his thighs in mud, but still barking. Still in control. Still telling me what to do. Now. Next. Now. *(To rifle:)* SO TELL ME!!!!!!

RIVERS: Stubbs, you won't believe this, but this one doesn't... *(Makes a writing movement)* ...either.

STUBBS: *(Doesn't hear her; to* GEORGIA:*)* JAM THAT BENCH AGAINST THE DOOR!!! *(Smiles)* I'm surprised by the strength of my voice. The bark of my voice.

*(*RIVERS *is now up and searching through her coat.)*

GEORGIA: *(Tapping* RIVERS *on the shoulder; trying to remain calm and above it all. She holds the coffee pot.)* Rivers, more coffee?

RIVERS: Leave me alone. Can't you see I'm busy?!!

STUBBS: *(To* GEORGIA*:)* DO IT!!

GEORGIA: *(Ignoring him, pours herself a cup; to* RIVERS*:)* Don't hesitate to help yourself, if you change your mind.

STUBBS: *(To himself:)* This the same voice. From the same brain. Which had been. Well, it had been shaking. Almost breaking, in fact. Almost ranting. Maybe this is now just another form of ranting. Maybe. Maybe. This taking charge just another way of giving up on myself. Trying to locate a more comfortable spot somewhere else. Inside someone else. Something else. Maybe. Maybe.

*(*GEORGIA *suddenly discovers a pencil near the telephone. She waves it at* RIVERS.*)*

GEORGIA: Rivers, look what I found.

RIVERS: *(To herself as she searches)* I don't believe this. What are the odds against this sort of thing happening?

STUBBS: WHERE IS THAT AMMUNITION BELT?!!!

GEORGIA: *(With pencil)* Rivers. Yoo-hoo. Rivers.

RIVERS: It's just not fair. One pen going dry, maybe. But two!

STUBBS: I find it. I find it myself on the arm of the couch. I throw it over my shoulder. I pat it as if it were alive. *(Pats the ammunition belt)*

GEORGIA: *(With pencil; insistent)* Rivers...!!

RIVERS: Will you get off my back!!!!

STUBBS: *(Yelling at* GEORGIA*:)* I TOLD YOU TO MOVE THAT BENCH!!!!

RIVERS: *(Seeing the pencil; screams:)* WHERE DID YOU GET THAT?!!! *(Grabs the pencil and begins to write)*

STUBBS: *(To himself)* I'm screaming now. That's just what I'm doing. But, shit, maybe I need to scream to shift gears. To move myself onto another thought. Think of what to do next. Now.

*(*GEORGIA *sits on couch. She tidies up the coffee table, fluffs up the pillows, etc. She ignores* STUBBS *and* RIVERS.*)*

STUBBS: Look, I'll keep the rifle. Rivers, you take the revolver. And, Georgia, you will be our extra pair of eyes. *(Turns away)* So that is what I'm thinking, is it? Not bad. Not half bad. I had no idea I had such a plan worked out. No idea. Jesus, I wonder what I'm gonna say next.

*(*GEORGIA *hums quietly to herself.* RIVERS *has picked up the revolver and holds it under her arm as she writes.)*

STUBBS: *(To* RIVERS *and* GEORGIA:*)* We'll stay at the window. Rivers, you take left. I'll stay right. And Georgia. Over there. OVER THERE! Get the fuck over there and keep one eye on the kitchen and scream your fucking lungs out if you hear so much as a peep. NOW, DAMN IT! DAMN IT, GET INTO POSITION!!!!

RIVERS: *(To* GEORGIA:*)* YOU HEARD HIM, MOVE IT!!!

*(*GEORGIA *hums and doesn't move.)*

STUBBS: And now I sigh. Now I step back. Step back and look around. Now I expect to find myself somehow feeling as if I'd finally climbed into a skin that will not shudder. Will not shred. But instead. Yeh. Instead. Get this. I find I can't help smiling at myself. Can't help wondering if all I am really doing now is just a fair. Just a decent. Just a pretty good impersonation. NO! NO!!!

*(*STUBBS *and* RIVERS *at their respective windows.* RIVERS *continues to write.)*

STUBBS: So I. Now. As if to try to prove myself wrong. To prove I have indeed been well cast. That I fit. Fit! That I belong in this skin. At this time. Under these conditions. Fit. I WANT TO. I WANT TO FIGHT!!!! *(He suddenly breaks the window with the butt of his rifle. Pause.)* But no. Oh shit. No. No. Instead of cementing. Instead of proving. Get this. The breaking glass only makes me shudder. Draws me back. And now. Now even worse I get it into my head. You won't believe this. I get it into my skull. Where first I'm wondering if it had really been necessary to break the window. I think that. Really. I think, how expensive a window is. Incredible. I don't believe it. How stupid. And now, second, I begin to see myself as small. As downright out of place. Out of my element. I begin to feel my age. And feel awkward. And I begin to see this whole thing. With the gun. With the window. With the barking. I begin to see it as a charade. And myself as embarrassing. As pointless. As sad.

And now I stand. Pull my rifle back. "My" rifle. What a joke. I stand. Very alone now. Very much alone. Very red in the face. Very ashamed of myself. WHAT AM I DOING?!! WHAT THE FUCK AM I DOING WITH THIS?!!!! *(He throws the rifle down. Covers his face. Pause. Then, suddenly "out of" the entry, he takes a pack of cigarettes out of pocket. To* RIVERS:*)* You want one? I found them in her purse.

*(*RIVERS *nods, finishes her writing.* STUBBS, *breathing heavily, lights their cigarettes. They smoke.)*

(Short pause)

STUBBS: Good scene.

*(*RIVERS *nods. Pause.)*

*(*GEORGIA *suddenly screams twice.* STUBBS *and* RIVERS *turn to her.)*

GEORGIA: You know what *I'm* doing? Do you? Huh? I'll bet you don't. I'll bet you haven't the faintest. Well, am I right? Or am I right? Well, I'm trying to shake it all up. All up in here. *(Points to her head)* Figure it couldn't hurt. No. No. Maybe the pieces will begin to fall into place. Up here. Couldn't hurt. Couldn't be worse. Could it? Huh? Huh? *(No response)* DO YOU KNOW WHAT IT FEELS LIKE?!!! *(To* RIVERS:*)* Do you? To be standing here. And you. Him. He starts up. He starts crying. He starts shoutin', do this. Do that. *(To* STUBBS:*)* And her. She's right with you. The two of you. And me. I keep thinking. Brother, I sure missed something. Brother, am I stupid. *(Stops. She screams.)* Nope. Still doesn't work. Still didn't shake nothin' into place.

But as I was saying. Brother, am I. Am I. What was I saying. WHAT THE HELL WAS I SAYING?!!!!!

STUBBS: *(Quiet, soothing voice:)* Go on. Go on.

GEORGIA: *(Screams again)* That's better. That's much better. So. Maybe it's because I'm not seeing things so good. What do you think? Possible? Is that possible? Maybe 'cause every time I close my eyes. See, I've closed them. And all I see is: bedroom. Is: blood. So maybe because my mind is. Is what? TELL ME!!! Maybe because of that. You. And her. It all seems so very very odd. Maybe that's why I'm feeling so. Right? Right? Do you think that explains it? Do you? Do you? Please, do you?! TELL ME! TELL ME! PLEASE, SOMEBODY TELL ME! !! *(She covers her face.)*

(Short pause)

*(*STUBBS *applauds,* RIVERS *join in.)*

STUBBS: Bravo. Bravissimo. Bravo.

*(*GEORGIA *looks up, crying.)*

GEORGIA: Huh?

STUBBS: *(Walks over to* GEORGIA, *pats her on the shoulder.)* Georgia. Nice. That was tremendously moving. *(He returns to his thinking.)*

RIVERS: *(Walks over to* GEORGIA*)* I'm touched. I'm deeply touched.

*(*RIVERS *hugs* GEORGIA, *turns, returns to her notebook.)*

GEORGIA: It...? *(No response)* It was...? *(No response)* It was really good?

(Blackout)

Scene Five

(Setting: The same.)

(Stage dark)

*(*STUBBS*, in black, begins to laugh, almost uncontrollably.)*

(Lights up)

*(*STUBBS *stands center.* GEORGIA *and* RIVERS *are on the couch watching him.* RIVERS *no longer takes notes.)*

STUBBS: *(Continuing with a "story": trying to hold back his laughter, though not succeeding very well)* And so. So for some reason. *(Laughs)* Some God knows why reason, I start to. Because the entire situation here. Them out. Out. This whole fucking picture. *(Laughs, giggles)* With Rivers there concerned. Looking very prim, see. With Georgia almost in. Almost in. In anguish. *(Laughs)* And the window. Let's not forget the window! And with my own face. No doubt. very stiff. Yes. Very serious face. This face. My face. *(Laughs; wipes the tears from his eyes)* So for some reason. It just all becomes hilarious. I don't know why. Just one great big. Big joke, see. That now. That now I'd somehow just been let in on. You see? *(Laughs)* Even though. One side of me. Angry. Yeh. Pissed as hell. Yeh. One side telling me: shut up. SHUT UP! But I can't. I can't. No way. Not for a million bucks. It's too. It's just all too. Why the hell not? It just all too funny now.... *(Laughs out of control. Suddenly stops. Calm. Out of his "story")*

*(*RIVERS *and* GEORGIA *applaud.)*

*(*STUBBS *sits on the couch.* RIVERS *stands, thinking, she clears her throat. She takes center stage.*

(Short pause.)

RIVERS: I'm confused. Or maybe. Better. I'm sort of at odds with myself. On the one hand, see, I want to try to figure out what there is that we *can* do. You know, maybe run for it. It's pretty dark out there. Or go out shooting. I don't know. Whatever. Something like that. But on the other hand, I feel like I should be doing just what I have been doing. Right here with you, Stubbs. Helping you. You know? After all, that is my job, isn't it?

(Short pause)

STUBBS: Start again. More...immediacy, I think. Know what I mean? It sounds like you have it all figured out.

RIVERS: Immediacy. *(Nods)* Okay. *(Clears hers throat. throws back her hair.)* I'm scared. That's here all right. My hands have been shaking so hard it's been difficult to write. Really. I keep hearing those gun shots. And somehow my fingers keep feeling for that revolver. I feel a chill. A chill that's so solid, so physical, it feels like a hit. A punch. A constant banging. Like a heavy cold shower. I can't seem to get comfortable. I want to work. I want to concentrate. After all. After all, that's my job. That's very important to me. But there still is this fear. I guess because of shooting. *Actually* firing. Because I really *did* pull the trigger. I guess 'cause I got started. And then. Then just stopped. Stopped and started waiting. So there's the sense of conclusions, you know, not yet having run their course. Not yet completed their cycle. That sense of an uncompleted motion. A half step. Start-stop. And all too sudden. And the waiting makes it worse. Like the action is still right there, I just gotta grab it. The action is just waiting for me to finish it. So the sense of being pulled at. Tugged at. This way. And that. Well, it sometimes has even felt like I was splitting apart. Like, see, I'm breaking in half. Then. Then it's real bad. What I'm feeling. Then, it's terrible. Then it's real bad. What I'm feeling. Then, it's terrible. It's a nightmare. Then: Jesus. JESUS CHRIST. STUBBS, IT'S SO GOD DAMN AWFUL, I CAN'T STAND IT!!!! (Breaks down. Short pause. It takes her a little while to get calm.)

(Applause)

*(*RIVERS *returns to the couch.)*

STUBBS: *(Takes* RIVERS' *hand and winks)* Better. Much better.

(She sits.)

*(*GEORGIA *stands, nervous.)*

GEORGIA: Well, I guess I feel, you know. Well, sort of privileged. In a way. After all, you're a Senator and I'm. Well, who the hell am *I*, you know?

*(*STUBBS *has been listening intently; snaps his fingers:* GEORGIA *stops; he goes to* GEORGIA, *almost whispers to her:)*

STUBBS: Look, Georgia. It is always obvious when one is faking the emotion. Do you understand? And when it is obvious, there is no interest. When there's no interest, no point. No point, then why do it? You understand?

(She nods. STUBBS *returns to the couch.)*

GEORGIA: I am feeling.... *(Short pause)* I guess I'm feeling, you know...resentful.

(She looks for a reaction, STUBBS *nods.)*

GEORGIA: I mean, well. You come into here. My house. This *is* my house. Where *I* live. And. And mostly you. But also her. You come into here and you keep doing this stuff. And I'm made to feel like I'm the one who is intruding. That I'm the one butting in. That I don't belong here.

And then. When we realize what's happened. When I'm frightened. When I keep thinking and I can't get it out of my mind, and I feel guilty even trying. Thinking that Winslow is dead. When, as you know too. When what happened to Winslow will probably happen to us, too. That all this isn't over. Not by any means. Not by a long shot. When all this has happened in my house. And in my head. And I turn and look for what? Maybe just a little tiny bit of concern. Of consolation. Not only because of Winslow. But also because we're all in this together. Stuck together, almost. No choice. Well, there should be, I keep telling myself. There should be some mutual concern. A certain togetherness. A "let's help each other" spirit. But you. You not only don't put your arm around me. Give me a shoulder to... But you make me feel like I'm fucking butting in. Like I should go away. Well, where should I go? WHERE THE HELL SHOULD I GO?!!!!!!

I don't know. See. It's all become like a dream. That I can't remember anymore. Nothing specific. Just this feeling. This aftertaste. But still. But I know it's still not over. So I keep pricking myself. Keep thinking, you are not really there. No. 'Cause if you were. If you were there, I wouldn't be feeling so much hate and disgust for you. So much resentment. I wouldn't be feeling like, even though I'm in my own god damn house, I'm stuck somewhere else. Some place I've never been before. Somewhere. Where I'm all alone.

(Short pause. GEORGIA, *close to tears, closes her eyes, not knowing what to expect.)*

*(*STUBBS *claps loudly.* RIVERS *applauds and whistles.)*

*(*GEORGIA *opens her eyes and smiles, pleased.)*

(The applause stops. GEORGIA *sits,* STUBBS *stands, thinking.)*

(Pause)

GEORGIA: Can I try one more?

(Blackout)

Scene Six

(Setting: The same.)

(Stage dark. Lights fade up.)

*(*STUBBS, GEORGIA, *and* RIVERS *are waiting. Each is doing something idiosyncratic, like clicking their nails, jiggling a foot, etc.* GEORGIA *also reads a book.* STUBBS *and* RIVERS *on the couch.* GEORGIA *is on the bench.)*

(Pause)

(Gun shot, off. The vase on the table explodes.)

(They are startled, jump.)

*(*GEORGIA *stands slowly. She drops her book. The others watch her. She does not look down. She fiddles with her bracelet. No expression on her face. Her hands shake.)*

GEORGIA: *(Finally:)* I keep seeing his face. I keep seeing Winslow's face up there. *(She starts to cry. She begins to take a step toward center but stops, covers her face, lowers her head, then raises her head slowly and suddenly screams.)*

STUBBS: *(Stands; angry:)* Oh fuck, I'm getting real tired of this. SHUT UP!!!

RIVERS: *(Holding him back)* Stubbs, she's upset.

STUBBS: Oh she is, is she. Well what do you think I am, huh? I'm upset too. ME TOO!! But least I make the effort to control myself. Make the effort to keep a lid on this. Keep myself together. LEAST I'M NOT SCREAMING EVERYONE'S BRAINS LOOSE!!

*(*GEORGIA *screams.)*

STUBBS: I SAID, STOP THAT!!

(He grabs at GEORGIA*'s arm. She turns toward him and spits in his face.* STUBBS *is taken aback but very angry now. He wants to hit her.* RIVERS *jumps up and grabs* STUBBS.*)*

RIVERS: Don't touch her, Stubbs! *(She pushes him away. To* GEORGIA*)* You shouldn't have done that, Georgia. *(Puts her arm around* GEORGIA*)* Hey, take it easy. Come on. Come on. It's all forgotten. There. There.

(Comforts her. GEORGIA *starts sobbing. Short pause)*

(Suddenly, everyone calm, they all nod at each other and return to their earlier positions. STUBBS *and* RIVERS *on the couch, etc.)*

(Pause)

(EXPLOSION off. Every one turns to the door. RIVERS *gets up and peeks out the window.)*

RIVERS: *(To* STUBBS*;)* Georgia's car's on fire.

GEORGIA: *("In shock")* What?! *My* car?!! *(She gets up and charges toward the window.)*

RIVERS: *(Trying to stop her)* Don't get too close.

*(*GEORGIA *fights to get away.)*

RIVERS: I said, don't get too close! Stop kicking!

*(*GEORGIA *bites her hand.)*

RIVERS: She bit me!! She bit me!!

*(*RIVERS *slaps her across the face,* GEORGIA *falls to the floor.* RIVERS *walks away, rubbing her hand.)*

STUBBS: *(To* RIVERS*:)* Let me see. *(Looks at her hand)* You'll live. *(Smacks her on the fanny. He goes over to* GEORGIA.*)* Georgia...

GEORGIA: *(Pointing toward the door)* But *my*...!

RIVERS: *(Rubbing her hand)* She broke the skin.

STUBBS: *(Giving* GEORGIA *his hand)* I know. I know.

(She takes it. He pulls her up. Short pause. They all "break", become calm, nod, pleased with each other, and return to their former positions. Pause)

GEORGIA: *(She starts to wipe her hands on her dress, then notices the blood. She tenses and mumbles:)* Those bastards.

STUBBS: What did you say, Georgia?

GEORGIA: Never mind.

STUBBS: Georgia, if you have something to say, you should say it.

RIVERS: Stubbs is right. Get it off your chest, Georgia. You'll feel better.

GEORGIA: *(Holding up part of her bloody dress)* I said, "Those bastards".

STUBBS: And how do you feel about those bastards? Do you hate them?

*(*GEORGIA *nods)*

STUBBS: Then say it like you do.

GEORGIA: *(With hate)* Those bastards!

STUBBS: You want to strangle them with your own hands, don't you?

GEORGIA: *(Nods; with more anger:)* Those bastards!!!

STUBBS: You want to tear their eyes out!

GEORGIA: *(Standing, yelling)* THOSE BASTARDS!!!!

STUBBS: That's it!

GEORGIA: *(She grabs a pillow from the couch and begins punching it and shouting:)* THOSE BASTARDS! THOSE BASTARDS!

STUBBS: THAT'S IT!! THAT'S IT!!

GEORGIA: *(Screams:)* THOSE GOD DAMN BASTARDS!!!!

(Short pause. They all "break", become calm, and return to their former positions. Pause.)

RIVERS: *(Finally:)* It's still your turn, Stubbs.

STUBBS: *(Suddenly angry)* DON'T YOU THINK I KNOW THAT!!! *(Calm:)* That felt nice.

(Pause)

GEORGIA: Did I tell you about what I was feeling in the car? When I was driving you two here?

STUBBS: *(To* RIVERS:*)* Did she?

*(*RIVERS *nods.)*

GEORGIA: Oh.

(Pause)

STUBBS: I feel nothing. Nothing. Not a thing. As if my emotions, so stretched. So strained. Have not bent, but broken. And so now, like maybe snapped ends of a wire, they lay limp. Unable to make any connection. ...That's a possibility. *(He thinks.)*

(Pause)

GEORGIA: Did I tell you about how I felt at your hotel? My frustration? My confusion? My pent-up anger?

STUBBS: Did she?

RIVERS: Yes.

GEORGIA: Oh. *(Pause)*

STUBBS: I feel...everything. All at once. A mess and a blur of feelings. Wires crossed... That's also a possibility. *(He thinks.)*

(Pause)

GEORGIA: Did I tell you about how I was feeling when those men out there called?

(STUBBS *turns to* RIVERS *as if to say "Did she?"* RIVERS *nods.)*

GEORGIA: Oh.

(Pause)

GEORGIA: Did I tell you about how I felt when I found Winslow?

STUBBS: Did she?

RIVERS: No.

(GEORGIA *slaps her hands together and takes center stage.* STUBBS *and* RIVERS *watch.)*

GEORGIA: Well. Well, see, I guess you could say I was already worried. See, I hadn't admitted it to myself, you know. The kind of worry that you only feel but don't allow yourself to think. I mean, after he wasn't in the kitchen. After I'd seen the roast still in the sink. I felt, well, I guess I even thought—"heart attack". I think I even said to myself: "heart attack". So, see, I was already pretty anxious when I started up the steps to the bedroom. I was already holding my breath and jumping for explanations. I was already seeing, you know, expecting to see a note on our bureau telling me he'd got a call from the office. And I was already angry at him for leaving and forgetting about the roast.

So, when I tried to open the door, and it was jammed. Not locked. But jammed so I could only open it a couple of inches. I had no thought. Nothing. This just didn't fit. What the hell could this have to do with that note on our bureau I kept "seeing". So I pushed. With all my strength. I pressed my shoulder against and pushed. And then.

And then—a foot. Only a foot. PUSH! PUSH, GEORGIA! HEART ATTACK!! PUSH!! Then—blood. Then as the door inched open. Then—

(Suddenly,gun shots rip a line of holes across the door.)

(Everyone turns to the door.)

*(*GEORGIA *steps upstage.)*

STUBBS: *(Quietly)* Here they come.

RIVERS: It won't be long now.

GEORGIA: I guess not.

STUBBS: *(Taking center stage)* Now, let me think—my last words. I am going to need some appropriate last words. *(He thinks. Short pause)*

RIVERS: Now that you mention it, Stubbs, I guess, so will I. *(She takes center. Short pause)*

GEORGIA: Me too. *(Takes center. Short pause)*

RIVERS: What about...? No. No. *(Short pause)*

STUBBS: I've got mine.... No. No. *(Short pause)*

GEORGIA: How does this sound.... Nah. *(Short pause)*

RIVERS: Uh. No. Too maudlin. *(Short pause)*

STUBBS: Yeh. Too clever. *(Short pause)*

GEORGIA: I have mine! Wait. I just lost it.... Shit, it's right on the tip of my tongue.... *(Short pause)*

(Gun shot blast—the door is shot off its hinges and crashes to the floor.)

(They all turn and look.)

(Blackout)

Scene Seven

(Setting: Vienna. Sitting room of a hotel suite. Same as Scene One.)

(Two years later)

(Stage dark. Lights up)

*(*RIVERS *sits on the chaise.* GUNTER *stands center.)*

GUNTER: It was a winter's evening, two years ago today, when a black American limousine sped through the narrow side streets of Vienna. In the back seat, the American senator thumbed through an issue of *The Herald Tribune*. He read the football scores first. And then the news. As he pressed his face to the window, he saw a cathedral. He noticed that the breath of the pedestrians created small clouds in the air. As they passed a Coca Cola sign, he smiled to himself. The senator sat back as the car lurched forward, headed for an intimate Viennese hotel. This hotel. Where upstairs, in Suite 812, a bald-headed man paced his room, avoiding every squeak in the floor.

Suddenly, this man stops and pulls back the lace window curtain. He looks down on the street below. He keeps the light off and one hand over part of his face. He turns the yellow knob of the radio and listens to a Strauss waltz. He smokes American cigarette after American cigarette. He waits.

The limousine glides up in front of the green awning of the hotel. I hurry outside and bow as a porter is trained to bow. That is, without much to do. The senator grips my shoulder and winks. The elevator jerks and squeaks, but the senator calls the ride smooth. His bags are of the softest leather. Other guests on the same floor have left their doors open just a crack. They wish to get a peek of the famous American senator. An inconspicuous peek.

One door, however, remains closed. The door to Suite 812. Where, inside, the bald headed man is practicing putting a drinking glass against a connecting door. The one which connects his room with Suite 814.

A couple of guests now find excuses to wander the hall. One says she is looking for her shoes. The senator slaps everyone on the back. He shakes two different hands at the same time. He retires to his suite. Number 814.

I return to the lobby. I find myself humming. Something by Liszt. I catch my reflection in a mirror which has a pattern in gold leaf. I wink at myself. I practice shaking two hands at the same time. I whistle "O Susannah".

But upstairs. The man in 812 has grabbed for a phone. He is dialing. The call is answered on the first ring. "The country!" He wants to scream, but forces out a whisper. "Yes, the country. Senator Stubbs will be having dinner in the country." And he hangs up. He lights the last of his American cigarettes. He pats the spot on his chest, making sure the bulge made of metal is still there. Weeks later, it would be learned that this man had been trained in the Middle East. That he was an expert with explosives. That his father was a retired schoolteacher from Burgenland. That his aunt writes poetry. And that his mother had died when he was twelve.

And so the course of events, which were soon to be played out in a farmhouse. With terrorists. With death. With fear. That course of events which would dominate the headlines and gossip of Vienna for weeks. Had been set in motion. It had begun. It had begun here. In this hotel. Right here! In suite 812. And in suite 814. Just two years ago today.

(Short pause. GUNTER *looks for a response.)*

RIVERS: *(Nods:)* Thank you, Gunter. Very charming. I will have the senator call you when he wakes up.

(Short pause. GUNTER *doesn't move.)*

RIVERS: Is there something else, Gunter?

*(*GUNTER *gestures with his head toward the pile of books on the desk.)*

RIVERS: Oh, of course! Of course, the book. How stupid of me to forget. By all means, Gunter, take a copy of the senator's memoirs. I'm sure he'd want you to have one. The top copy, yes. I believe that one is already signed.

*(*GUNTER *takes a copy and checks to see if it is signed.)*

RIVERS: And thank you again, Gunter, for that very lovely story. The senator will be thrilled to learn that he has become part of the history of this hotel.

*(*GUNTER *exits with book.)*

*(*STUBBS *enters from the bedroom. His hair disheveled; he wears a smoking jacket; he holds a large new book—his published memoirs.)*

RIVERS: Stubbs, don't you think Gunter is cute?

STUBBS: Who?

RIVERS: Gunter. The porter. He just told me the cutest little story.

STUBBS: Forget Gunter and tell me what you think about the election night story.

RIVERS: About the what?

STUBBS: I'm thinking of giving it for the lecture tonight. You think there'd be interest in that kind of thing?

RIVERS: The election night story? But I thought you were going to do our rescue story. I even think that's what they're counting on, Stubbs.

STUBBS: Forget that. And just tell me if you think they'll go for this. *(Opens the book)*

RIVERS: But, Stubbs, they have even named the lecture series after Georgia. You know, as sort of a memorial. Wait a minute, I think I've got the flyer here somewhere.

STUBBS: Look. I know what happened. You know what happened. They know what happened. I'm tired of that story. You're tired of that story, and, damn it, I'll bet they're just as tired of it too. So let's just forget it, okay?

RIVERS: Tired of it? What with us having given up hope. What with guns blazing. And bullets everywhere. And fire and smoke so you couldn't see you hand in front of your face. What with the two of us behind the couch. You patting my head. And me. I'm shaking like a. And Georgia! Georgia! Where the hell is she?! Georgia! We're screaming. We're choking. When suddenly, outside, we begin to hear...

STUBBS: *(Cuts her off)* Rivers, come on, I'm sick of telling it, okay? Come on and listen to this.

RIVERS: Sure, Stubbs. If that's what you want.

STUBBS: Well, that is what I want. Now just tell me whether you think they're gonna go for this. ...Where the hell are my glasses.

RIVERS: I'll check the bedrooms. *(Gets up)*

STUBBS: No. Why the hell don't you read it. That might be interesting. Maybe I can hear it better that way and be able to tell myself whether it'll play or not. Here. *(Hands her the book)* Where it's marked.

RIVERS: "Election night. I was in my suite"?

STUBBS: That's it. I'll stand back here. So it's more like it'll be. You ready?

(She nods)

STUBBS: Then, let's hear it. And for God's sake take your time. This ain't a race, okay?

RIVERS: Okay. *(Short pause; she clears her throat; reads:)* "Election night. I was in my suite at the Hotel Pierre. Three televisions were set in front of me. One for each network. I lounged with my shoes off on the couch. Friends, supporters, news people made a steady stream past me. I felt like I was holding some sort of court. I remember laughing to myself at the thought. I stretched my legs out but just couldn't get comfortable. I tried to eat, but my stomach already felt full. That's how tense I was. Trying to relax, I took a shower. But still felt dirty. I felt like I smelled as soon as I toweled myself off. I put my shoes back on so I'd feel like I didn't have to relax. That I wouldn't feel pressured to relax.

"The first returns had come hours before. A small town in Vermont. I won the town by twenty-three votes. And made a joke about it. Something like,"Now we just gotta run even." Everyone laughed. Real hard.

"As the East Coast states started to come in. I surprised everyone by going to bed. I'm playing this cool, I thought. I wondered if I'd wake up the President. Or a loser. When I did wake up, I thought I'd been asleep for hours, but it'd been only seconds. My sense of time was all warped. I felt a little bit foolish when I returned to the televisions so soon. But we all just laughed about it. Real hard.

"As the network projections were being flashed state by state, I got into the differing graphics of the three stations. One gave the percentage inside an American flag. Another within a group of stars. And the third had the map of the state that was in question. I thought about what I'd have chosen if the graphics were my job. I didn't come up with much.

"By midnight we were neck and neck. It was becoming obvious that California would be the big casino. One roll. One very big roll of the dice. It'd come down to that. I tried to name all the cities in California that I'd visited. I gave up after thirty. That's enough, I thought. You should have no regrets. So we all relaxed because we knew California wouldn't be final for a couple of hours. We all breathed easy. Getting ourselves set to start that slow move to the edge of our chairs as the minutes began to tick away. For the first time that night, I took a drink. I told myself I'd just sip it slowly. Make it last until California.

"But then. I never even had the chance to take a drop. Because. Because suddenly it was flashed! Ohio had changed hands! We'd lost it! We'd won it and now we'd lost it! There'd been a mistake. A big mistake. It was suddenly. What happened? WHAT HAPPENED?!! IT WAS OVER! IT WAS OVER! California wasn't enough. WE NEEDED OHIO!!!!!! *(Short pause. She is very "into" the story. Almost has to fight back tears)*

"I couldn't think of anything to do. I couldn't think of anything I wanted to do. Except *not* cry. Not cry like *they* were. Like everyone around me was. My actions, then, they became *not* actions. Do you see what I mean? I was *not* going to give up. I was *not* going to bed. I was *not* going to break down. I was *not* going to win". *(She shuts the book; takes a handkerchief and wipes her eyes. Pause)*

STUBBS: *(Half-smile)* I. I really do feel for that man. And so will they. It will play. It will play. It will play.

(Blackout)

END OF PLAY